Fanny Fern

Caper-Sauce

A Volume of Chit-Chat about Men, Women, and Things

Fanny Fern

Caper-Sauce
A Volume of Chit-Chat about Men, Women, and Things

ISBN/EAN: 9783744652797

Printed in Europe, USA, Canada, Australia, Japan

Cover: Foto ©ninafisch / pixelio.de

More available books at **www.hansebooks.com**

NEW BOOKS
BY
FANNY FERN.

---o---

I. — FOLLY AS IT FLIES . PRICE $1.50
II. — GINGER-SNAPS . . $1.50
III. — CA'PER-SAUCE . . $1.50

---o---

These volumes are all elegantly printed and bound in cloth : are sold everywhere, and will be sent by mail free of postage, on receipt of price,

BY

Carleton, Publisher,

New York.

A VOLUME OF CHIT-CHAT

ABOUT

MEN, WOMEN, AND THINGS.

BY

FANNY FERN,

AUTHOR OF

"FOLLY AS IT FLIES," "GINGER-SNAPS," "FERN LEAVES," ETC.

NEW YORK:

G. W. Carleton & Co., Publishers.

LONDON: S. LOW, SON & CO.

M.DCCC.LXXII.

Entered, according to Act of Congress, in the year 1872, by
G. W. CARLETON & CO.,
In the Office of the Librarian of Congress, at Washington.

Stereotyped at the
WOMEN'S PRINTING HOUSE,
56, 58 and 60 Park Street,
New York.

PREFACE.

EXCUSE me. None this time. There have already been too many big porticos before little buildings.

FANNY FERN.

NEW YORK, 1872.

M174961

CONTENTS.

	PAGE
Editors	9
My Notion of Music	16
"Budding Spring"—In the City	20
A Peep at Boston	23
Blackwell's Island	29
Shall we have Male or Female Clerks?	37
Unknown Acquaintances	40
Life and its Mysteries	44
Mrs. Washington's Eternal Knitting	47
The Woman Question	50
Two Kinds of Wives	55
Undertakers' Signs on Churches	58
A Voice from the Skating Pond	61
The Sin of being Sick	64
Are Ministers Serfs?	69
Blaming Providence for Our Own Faults	72
A Chapter on Nurses	74
Do American Women Love Nature?	78
Rainy-day Pleasures	82
Chit-Chat with Some of My Correspondents	84
My Liking for Pretty Things	92
Unsought Happiness	95
Dignity of Human Nature	100
All About Doctors	104
Letter to Henry Ward Beecher	108
The Amenities of the Table	111
Many Men of Many Minds	115
My Notion of a Walking Companion	118
Men Teachers in Girls' Schools	121
My Call on "Dexter"	125
The Poetry of Work	128
Can't Keep a Hotel	132

Contents.

	PAGE
New Clothes	136
How I read the Morning Papers	139
Betty's Soliloquy	143
My Dreadful Bump of Order	146
"Every Family Should Have It"	153
Getting to Rights	157
Modern Martyrs	163
Writing "Compositions"	168
Nice Little Tea-Parties	173
A Sleepless Night	176
Women's Need of Recreation	180
The Good Old Hymns	185
A Stranger in Gotham	189
My Journey to Quebec and Back Again	191
Idle Hours at Our Own Emerald Isle, the Gem of the Sea	215
Some City Sights	223
Dog-days in the Mountains	229
Spring in the City	235
Waifs	238
Tact	240
The Infirmities of Genius	242
A Trip to the Caatskills	245
The Trip to Brompton	258
Lake George Revisited	264
Cookery and Tailoring	269
Up the Hudson	273
"Why Don't I Lecture"	278
In the Cars	281
Petting	284
My Grievance	287
Cemetery Musings	290
The Scrubbing-brush Mania	292
Sauce for the Gander	295
My First Convert	298
Country Housewives	300
First Morning in the Country	303
Conscience Killing	306
The Cry of a Victim	308
Stones for Bread	311

CAPER-SAUCE.

EDITORS.

I AM not disposed to pity Editors. On the whole, I think they have a very good time. That national sugar-plum for American boys, "Maybe, my son, you will be one day *President*," might be changed advantageously for "My son, you may live some day to be an Editor." As for the *present* President, if he can sleep o' nights, he can live through anything! I repeat it, Editors have a good time, no matter what they say to the contrary. In the first place, I know that the position of an editor, if honorably filled, is second to none in this country. He need envy no one his influential power; would that in many cases it were more conscientiously wielded. If an *Editor* is an ignorant man, it is his own fault, no matter from what small beginnings he may have risen. Coming in contact, as he does, with information every instant, on all the absorbing topics of the day, it is next to impossible he should not be well informed. Read he must, whether he will or not. Think on what he has read he must; tell his subscribers, in words, what he thinks about it, and reflect and decide upon the submitted thoughts of others for his columns, he must. Hence the mind of an Editor is, or may be, a perfect Encyclopedia of information.

Of course he has his peculiar botherations; it would be a blessing if his subscription list were large enough for him to say just what he pleases right and left, without fear or favor. It would be a blessing if his subscribers would always pay punctually, without dunning. It would be a blessing, when he uses superhuman efforts to please them, if they never would find fault or grumble, for the sake of grumbling. It would be a blessing if they wouldn't stay so long when they come in to see him "just a minute," and he is in a frenzied hurry to say do go, and can't. It would be a blessing (to those who apply) if he could publish and pay for, at the valuation of the writers, all the immortal trash that is offered. It would be a blessing if other editors, "who can see nothing in his paper," wouldn't steal his articles constantly—editorial and contributed—without credit.

But, on the contrary, how came that beautiful bouquet on his desk? Where that fine engraving on his office wall? How came that beautiful picture and convenient inkstand there? I'd have you to know that the donors have not always an axe they wish to grind in that office. I dare say you will try to make me believe that Editors are human. Now

I deny that, for I myself have, in past days, had evidence to the contrary. But never mind that now. You may tell me that Editors are not above the weakness of publicly and slyly slipping in a good word for a good friend, when he needs it, and that they are not above giving a bad " friend " a good, satisfying dig when he needs it, and so would you. If a man is to be overhauled for.that, there's got to be a monstrous overturning of matters in other places beside Editors' offices. I confess I sometimes covet the quantities of books he accumulates free gratis for his library, and I should like to be allowed to review some of 'em after a fashion of my own, if nobody knew who did it; and I should like occasionally to dust their horrible desks for the poor creatures, and open those hermetically sealed windows, and advise them not to make themselves prematurely bald by wearing their hats in their offices, week in and week out, as if it were necessary their ideas should be kept warm like chickens in order to hatch.

Only that I am convinced that everybody must work in his own way, and that if Editors had to work in a clean place, they couldn't work at all. Now if they opened their office windows of a hot day, they might possibly be cooler, and a cool Editor, in times like these, when all the fire and fury we could master would not begin to express our national emotions, you see for yourself the thing wouldn't be tolerated. Beside, some of them ought to be getting used to a hot place, and they might as well begin now.

I wonder are Editors aware of how much importance is their Poet's corner! I wonder if they know that the most inveterate pursuer of brooms and gridirons that ever kept a good man's house tidy, likes a bit of sentiment, in that shape, in the family paper. I wonder do Editors know, how, when the day's work is done, she likes to pull that paper out from some old tea-caddy, or broken flower-pot—that long ago fell into disuse, and seating herself with a long-drawn breath of relief in the old-fashioned chair, where all her Tommys and Marys have been rocked, give herself up to the quiet enjoyment of its pages. Presently, as she reads, a tear gathers in her eye; she dashes it quickly away with an "ah—me," and laying her head back upon the chair, and closing eyes that were once much bluer than now, she is soon far, far away from the quiet home where her treadmill round of everyday duties has been for many years so faithfully performed, and, perhaps, alas! so thanklessly accepted. The cat comes purring round her feet, and Tray comes scratching at the door, but she does not move, till the sound of a heavy and familiar footstep is heard in the entry or hall; then, starting up, and taking her scissors from the long pocket at her side, she clips the precious verses from the paper and hides them in her bosom. Perhaps *you* might turn up your critical nose at those verses; never mind, they have touched *her* heart; and many times, when she is alone, she will read them over; and so long as they hold together, she will keep them in a little needle-case in her work-box, to read when "things go wrong," and a good, safe cry will ease the heart.

Her good man picks up the mutilated paper, and she says, "It was only a bit of poetry, John." Now, there are more Johns than one in the world, but he don't think of *that*, as turning to some political article he says, "Oh, you are quite welcome to all that sort of stuff;" nor does he know how much that other John had to do with her crying over those verses, which somebody certainly must have written, who, like herself, had married the wrong John.

Now, gentlemen Editors, crowd what else you may out of your papers, but *don't crowd out the poetry, or think it of small consequence.* Take the affidavit of one who has seen the clipped verses from your papers hid away in pocket-books, tucked away in needle-cases, speared upon pin-cushions, pinned up on toilet glasses, and murmured over in the mystic hour of twilight, just before "*John comes home to tea;*" and always have a bit of poetry in your columns for her who has so potent a voice in the choice of a family paper. I publicly promulgate this bit of wisdom, though I am very well aware that you will pass it off for your own, and neither credit *me* nor my book for it!

A word on a practice too common in some newspapers. I refer to the flippant manner in which the misfortunes and misdemeanors of certain classes, brought to the notice of our courts, are reported for the amusement of the community at large. Surely, it is melancholy enough that a drunken mother should be picked up in the gutter with her unconscious babe; or a young girl, scarcely in her teens, be found guilty of theft; or, that a husband and father should beat or murder her whom he had sworn to cherish, without narrating it after this heartless fashion. For instance:

John Flaherty, after beautifully painting a black and blue rim round his wife's eyes, was brought into court this morning to answer the question why he preferred that particular color; and not being able to give a satisfactory reason for the same, he was treated to a pleasant little ride to a stone building, where he was accommodated with a private room, board and lodging included.

Or thus:

Mary Honoria, scarlet-lipped, plump, and sweet sixteen, being fond of jewelry on her pretty person, and having stolen her mistress's watch, was waited upon by a gallant policeman, who escorted her little ladyship into court, in the presence of an admiring crowd, before whom her black eyes sparkled with a rage that but added new beauty to their lustre.

Now, I protest against this disgusting, demoralizing, and heartless mention of the sins and follies of poor wretches, the temptations of whose lot are as the sands of the sea-shore for multitude; who, ill-paid, ill-fed, worse-lodged, disheartened, discouraged, fall victims to the snares, in the shape of low groggeries, set for them by the very men who laugh over *their* well-spread breakfast tables, at this pitiful and revolting recital of their success. *Oh, write over against the poor wretch's name, as God does, why he or she fell!* or at least cease making it the subject for a jeer. Make it *your* son, *your* daughter, and then pen that flippant, heartless paragraph if you can. And yet, it was somebody's son, or daughter, or sister, or husband, unworthy it may be, (who is not?) but alas! often forgiven, and still dearly loved, to whose home that paragraph may come like a poisoned arrow, wounding the innocent, paralyzing the hand which was powerless enough before to struggle with its hapless fate; for not on the guilty does such blight fall heaviest. The young boy—the toiling, unprotected daughter—the aged mother—ah! what if they were *yours?*

About Doctors.—We wish doctors could ever agree. One's head gets muddled, reading their books on health, by antagonistic opinions on the same subject, from eminent sources. Experience is an excellent doctor, though he never had a diploma. What is good for you, you know is good for *you* although it may not be good for another. There is one point on which doctors all agree, and that is, they very rarely give physic to their own families. Why not? A friend suggests that it is from sheer benevolence, in order that they may have more left for other people.

MY NOTION OF MUSIC.

I'VE been defending myself from the charge of "not knowing what music is." Perhaps I don't know. But when I go to a fashionable concert, and the lady "*artiste*," I believe that is the regulation-word, comes out in her best bib and tucker, with a gilt battle-axe in her back hair, and a sun-flower in her bosom, led by the tips of her white gloves, by the light of a gleaming bracelet, and stands there twiddling a sheet of music, preparatory to the initiatory scream, I feel like screaming myself. Now if she would just trot on, in her morning gown, darning a pair of stockings, and sit naturally down in her old rocking-chair, and give me "Auld Robin Gray," instead of running her voice up and down the scales for an hour to show me how high and how low she can go without dropping down in a fit, I'd like it. One trial of her voice that way, to test its capacity, satisfies me. It is as good as a dozen, and a great deal better. I don't want to listen to it a whole evening. I *will* persist, that running up and down the scales that way isn't "*music*." Then if you only knew the agony I'm in, when drawing near the end of one of her musical gymnastics, she essays to wind up with one of those swift, deafening *don't-stop-to-breathe finales*, you *would* pity me. I get hysterical. I wish she would split her throat at once, or stop. I want to be let out. I want the roof lifted; I feel a cold perspiration breaking out on my forehead. I know that presently she will catch up that blue-gauze skirt and skim out that side-door, only to come and do it all over again, in obedience to that dead-head encore. You see all this machinery disenchants me. It takes away my appetite, like telling me at dinner how much beef is a pound. I had rather the ropes and pulleys of music would keep *behind* the curtain.

Of course my "taste is not cultivated," and moreover, the longer I live the less chance there is of it. On that point, I'm what country folks call "sot." Sometimes, when passing one of these concert-rooms of an evening, I *have* caught a note that I took home with me. Caught it with the help of the darkness and the glimmering stars, and the fresh wind on my forehead, and a blessed ignorance of the distorted mouth and the heaving millinery that sent it forth. But take me *in,* and you'll have an hysterical maniac. The solemn regulation faces, *looking* at that "music," set me bewitched to laugh and outrage that fashion-drilled and kidded audience. Bless you, *I* can't help it. I had rather hear Dinah sing "Old John Brown" over her wash-tub. I had rather go over to Mr. Beecher's church some Sunday night and hear that vast congregation swell forth Old Hundred, with each man and woman's *soul* so in it, that earthly cares and frets are no more remembered, than the old garments we cast out of sight.

When the words of a favorite hymn are read from the pulpit, and I am expecting the good old-fashioned tune, that has been wedded to it since my earliest recollection, and instead, I am treated to a series of quirks and quavers by a professional quartette, I can't help wishing myself where the whole congregation sing with the heart and the understanding, in the old-fashioned manner. I can have "opera" on week-days, and scenery and fine dresses thrown in. Sunday I want Sunday, not opera in *negligé*.

Of course it is high treason for me to make such an avowal; so, while I am in for it, I may as well give another twist to the rope that is round my neck. The other night I went to hear "The Messiah." The words are lovely, and as familiar to my Puritan ears as the "Assembly's Catechism;" but when they kept on repeating, "The Lord is in his hol—the Lord is in—is in his hol—is in—the Lord is in his hol"—and when the leader, slim, and clothed in inky black, kept his arms going like a Jack in a box, I grew anything but devout. The ludicrous side of it got the better of me; and when my companion, who pretends to be no Christian at all, turned to me, who am reputed to be one, in a state of exaltation, and said, "Isn't that grand, Fanny?" he could have wished that the tears in my eyes were not hysterical, from long-suppressed laughter. He says he never will take me there again, and I only hope he will keep his word. All the "music" I got out of it was in one or two lovely "solos."

Now what I want to know is, which has the most love for *genuine* music—he or I?

The fact is, I like to find my music in unexpected, simple ways, where the machinery is not visible, like the Galvanic gyrations of that "leader," for instance. That kind of thing recalls too vividly my old "fa-sol-la" singing-school, where the boys pulled my curls, and gave me candy and misspelt notes.

There is evidently something wanting in my make-up, with regard to "music," when I can *cry* at the singing of the following simple verses, by the whole congregation in church, and do the opposite at the scientific performance of "The Messiah." Listen to the verses:

> "Pass me not, O gentle Saviour,
>   Hear my humble cry;
> While on others Thou art smiling,
>   Do not pass me by.
>   Saviour, Saviour,
>   Hear my humble cry.
>
> "If I ask Him to receive me,
>   Will he say me Nay?
> Not till earth and not till heaven
>   Shall have passed away."

"BUDDING SPRING"—IN THE CITY.

WE of the city do not appreciate the blessing of closed windows and silence, until budding Spring comes. The terrific war-whoop of the milkman inaugurates the new-born day long before we should otherwise recognize it. Following him is the rag-man, with his handcart, to which six huge jangling, terrific cow-bells are fastened, as an accompaniment to the yet louder yell of "r-a-g-s." Then comes the " S-t-r-a-w-b-e-r-r-y " man, with lungs of leather, splitting your head, as you try to sip your coffee in peace. Close upon his heels, before he has hardly turned the corner, comes the pine-apple man, who tries to outscreech *him*. Then the fishman, who blows a hideous tin trumpet, loud enough to rouse the Seven Sleepers, and discordant enough to set all your nerves jangling, if they had not already been taxed to the utmost. You jump up in a frenzy to close the window, only to see that the fishman has stopped his abominable cart at the door of a neighbor, who keeps a carriage and livery, and is therefore fond of cheap, stale fish; where he is deliberately cleaning and splitting them, and throwing the refuse matter in the street, as a bouquet for your nostrils during the warm day. Then comes a procession of heavy carts, the drivers of which are lashing their skeleton nags to fury, with loud cracks of their whips, to see which shall win in the race, while every one of your window-panes shakes as if an earthquake were in progress, as they rumble over the stones. By this time comes a great mob of boys, with vigorous lungs, tossing each other's caps in the air, and screeching with a power perfectly inexplicable at only six, ten, or twelve years of practice. Indeed, the smaller the boy the bigger is his war-whoop, as a general rule. Then comes a wheezy organ-grinder, who, encouraged by the fatal show of plants in your windows, imagines you to be romantically fond of "The Morning Star," and immediately begins, in verse, to describe how he "feels." Nothing short of fifty cents will purchase his absence, which encouragement is followed by some miserable little rats of boys, anxious to succeed him on the violin and harp.

By this time your hair stands on end, and beads of perspiration form upon your nose. You fly for refuge to the back of the house. Alas! there is a young thing of "sixteen summers" and no winters running up and down the gamut on a tin-kettle piano. In the next house is a little dog barking as if his last hour was coming; while upon the shed are two cats, in the most inflamed state of bristle, glaring like fiends, and "*maow*"-ing in the most hellish manner at each other's whiskers. You go down into the parlor, and seat yourself there.

Your neighbor, Tom Snooks, is smoking at his window, and puffing it right through yours over your lovely roses, the perfume of which he quite extinguishes with his nasty odor.

Heavens! And this is "Spring!" "Budding Spring!" The poets make no mention of these little things in their "Odes!"

Well—at least, you say to yourself, there will be peace and heavenly quiet with the stars at midnight, by the open window. I will be patient till then.

Is there?

What is that? A policeman's loud rap-rap on the pavement for assistance to capture a burglar. Next a woman's scream; the brute who just accosted the poor wretch has struck her a heavy blow upon the temple. And now reels past a drunken man, zigzagging down the street, with a little whimpering boy by one hand, old enough to know what a "Station-house" means, and trembling lest "father" should be taken there.

You throw yourself upon your bed, weary and sick at heart. Even the stars seem to glow with a red, unnatural light, as if they too were worn with watching the wrongs and frets they nightly look down upon.

"Balmy night." What liars poets can be!

A PEEP AT BOSTON.

BOSTON is a lovely place to be baptized in, and to go back to. My old love, "*Boston Common*"—that good, old-fashioned, unspoiled, unmodernized name—looks more lovely this summer than I ever remember to have seen it. New York may well take a lesson from its order and neatness, with regard to our ill-kept *city* parks. I sat there, under those lovely trees which used to wave over my school-girl head; and had it not been for the little bright-eyed grandchild beside me picking buttercups, I might have fancied it was Saturday afternoon, and no school, and that I was to be back to my mother's apronstrings "by sundown, without fail." I know I could not have enjoyed even then the birds' song, or the sparkling pond, or the big trees more than at that moment. Out of my dream-land, whither they had led me, I was awakened by a jump into my lap, and the question, "And did you *really* play with buttercups here, when you were a little girl?" It was a long bridge that question led me over, so long that I forgot to answer till the question was repeated. I had to stop, and outgrow buttercups, and hold again by my matronly hand a little creature, the counterpart of my questioner, who long since closed her eyes forever, in this world, upon us both! It took time, you see, before I could say, "Yes, dear; it was just in this very lovely spot that both your mother and I picked buttercups when children, on the bright Saturday afternoons of long ago; and six years and a half of your little life I have waited, to see *you* run down those sloping paths, and to show you the 'Frog-Pond,' and to tell you to look up into the branches that nearly touch the sky; and now here we are! But there were no 'deer' feeding on this Common when I was a little girl, but instead *cows* to whom I gave plenty of room to pass as I went along; and instead of that gay little hat, with mimic grasses and daisies, such as I have put upon your head, my mother tied under my chin a little sun-bonnet. And she didn't run to me if I sneezed, as I do to you, for I had a heap of brothers and sisters, and we had to take care of our own sneezing; but I know I had twenty-five cents to spend on Fourth of July; and I know that, if any little girl's belt in Boston was ever tightened by roast turkey and pie more than mine was on 'Thanksgiving day,' I pity her! I wonder what has become of all the little children I used to play with here? We used to go up to the tip-top of that State House, I know; but I don't care to try it now. Not that it would tire me—of course not; but I've seen all that can be seen from that dome, and a little farther too."

Oh, the peace and loveliness of sweet "Mount Auburn!" The new graves since I was there, and the old graves now moss-grown that I remember so well! I, too, shall sleep sweetly there some day; but the hardest pang I shall know, between now and then, will be letting go the little hand that clasped mine to-day, as I walked about there. And yet there were *little* graves all around us. *He* knows best!

In Boston I saw the remains of "The Jubilee." I was asked, "Did I hear and see the Jubilee?" I was supposed, as coming from New York, to grieve at the success of "The Jubilee;" and being an adopted New Yorker, to feel like skulking round the back streets in Boston, covered with confusion that Manhattan had no "Jubilee." Lord bless you! I love every *bean* that was ever baked in Boston; every cod-fish-ball ever fried; and every brown-bread loaf ever baked there. I know too, as well as any Bostonian, that—

> "Zaccheus he
> Did climb the tree,
> His Lord and Master
> For to see;"

and I made a courtesy to the ground, when I came in sight of "Park-street" steeple, and "Faneuil Hall!" so don't be pitching into me. Hit some other fellow who isn't "up" in the Assembly's catechism, and "total depravity," and brown bread. "Jubilee" as much as you want to; the world is a big place. "Holler" away!

New England, all hail to thy peerless thrift! Thou art cranky and crotchety; thou art "sot," uncommon "sot," in thy ways, owing doubtless to the amiable sediment of English blood in thy veins. Thou wilt not be cheated in a bargain, even by thy best friend; but, in the meantime, that enableth thy large heart to give handsomely when charity knocks at thy door. Thy pronunciation may be peculiar, but, in the meantime, what thou dost not know, and cannot do, is rarely worth knowing or doing. Thou never hast marble, and silver, and plate glass, and statuary, in thy show-parlors, and shabby belongings where the world does not penetrate. Thou hast not stuccoed walls, with big cracks in them, or anything in thy domiciles, hanging as it were by the eyelids. Every nail is driven so that it will stay; every hinge hung so that it will work thoroughly. Every bolt and key and lock perform their duty like a martinet, so long as a piece of them endures. If thou hast a garden, be it only a square foot, it is made the most of with its "long *saace*," and "short *saace*," and "wimmin's notions," in the shape of flowers and caraway seed, to chew on Sunday, when the minister gets as far as "seventeenthly," and carnal nature will fondly recur to the waiting pot of baked beans in the kitchen oven. O! New England, here could I shed salt tears at the thought of thy baked beans, for Gotham knows them not. Alluding to that edible, I am met with a pitying sneer, accompanied with that dread word to snobs—"*provincial!*" It is ever thus, my peerless, with the envy which cannot attain to the perfection it derides. For you should see, my thrifty New England, the watery, white-livered, tasteless, swimmy, sticky poultice which Gotham christens "baked beans." My soul revolts at it. It is an unfeeling, wretched mockery of the rich, brown, crispy, succulent contents of that "platter"—yes, *platter*—I will say it!—which erst delighted my eyes in the days when I swallowed the Catechism without a question as to its infallibility. The flavor of the beans "haunts memory still;" but as to the Catechism, the world is progressing, and I am not one to put a drag on its wheels, believing that

    Truth is sure
    And will endure,

and it is best to let "natur" caper, especially as you can't help it; and after the dust it has kicked up has cleared away, we shall see what we shall see, be it wheat or chaff. Beside, the most conservative must admit, that though Noah's Ark was excellent for the flood, the "Great Eastern" is an improvement on it; and *'tisn't* pretty, *so they say who oftenest practise it!* to stand with the Bible in your hand in 1862, and clamor for a private latch-key to heaven.

But I have wandered from my baked beans. I want some. Some New England baked beans. Some of "mother's beans." But, alas, mother's oven is fast disappearing. Mother's oven, where the beans stayed in all night, with the brown bread. Alas! it has given way to new-fangled "ranges," which "don't know beans." Excuse the vulgarity of the expression, but in such a cause I shan't stand for trifles. If you want rose-leaf sentimental-refinement, together with creamy patriotism, you may look in the columns of the Whip-Syllabub-Family-Visitor. This is a digression.

When I started for a New England tour, it was my intention to get some of those beans; but the hotels there are getting so "genteel" with their paper-pantalettes on the roast-chicken's legs, and their paper frills on the roast-pigs'-tails, that I was convinced, that only at a genuine unsophisticated farm-house, where I could light down unannounced on Sarah-Jane—could this edible in its native and luscious beauty be found.

Next summer, if "strategy" and the rebels don't chew us up, I start on a tour for those beans; nor am I to be imposed upon by any "genteel" substitutes or abortions under that name!

A Hint to Parents.—When parents are considering the question of the hours of study for growing children in our schools, let them do it without any reference to the side question, how they can "bear those noisy children, during the subtracted hours, at home." Perhaps they can better bear this than to pay the doctor's bills. This is the way to look at it, whether it be regarded in a selfish or a humanitarian point of view.

BLACKWELL'S ISLAND.

PRIOR to visiting Blackwell's Island, my ideas of that place were very forlorn and small-pox-y. It makes very little difference, to be sure, to a man, or a woman, shut up in a cell eight feet by four, how lovely are the out-door surroundings; how blue the river that plashes against the garden wall below, flecked with white sails, and alive with gay pleasure-seekers, whose merry laugh has no monotone of sadness, that the convict wears the badge of degradation; and yet, after all, one involuntarily says to one's self, so instinctively do we turn to the cheerful side, I am glad they are located on this lovely island. Do you shrug your shoulders, Sir Cynic, and number over the crimes they have committed? Are *your* crimes against society less, that they are written down only in God's book of remembrance? Are *you* less guilty that you have been politic enough to commit only those that a short-sighted, unequal human law sanctions? Shall I pity these poor wrecks of humanity less, because they are so recklessly self-wrecked? because they turn away from my pity? Before I come to this, I must know, as their Maker knows, what evil influences have encircled their cradles. How many times, when their stomachs have been empty, some full-fed, whining disciple, has presented them with a Bible or a Tract, saying, "Be ye warmed and filled." I must know how often, when their feet have tried to climb the narrow, up-hill path of right, the eyes that have watched, have watched only for their halting; never noting, as God notes, the steps that did *not* slip—never holding out the strong right hand of help when the devil with a full larder was tugging furiously at their skirts to pull them backward; but only saying "I told you so," when he, laughing at your pharisaical stupidity, succeeded.

I must go a great way back of those hard, defiant faces, where hate of their kind seems indelibly burnt in; back—back—to the soft blue sky of infancy, overclouded before the little one had strength to contend with the flashing lightning and pealing thunder of misfortune and poverty which stunned and blinded his moral perceptions. I cannot see that mournful procession of men, filing off into those dark cells, none too dark, none too narrow, alas! to admit troops of devils, without wishing that some white-winged angel might enter too; and when their shining eyeballs peer at my retreating figure through the gratings, my heart shrieks out in its pain—oh! believe that there is pity here—only pity; and I hate the bolts and bars, and I say this is *not* the way to make bad men good; or, at least if it be, these convicts should not, when discharged, be thrust out loose into the world with empty pockets, and a bad name, to earn a speedy "through-ticket" back again. I say, if this *be* the way, let humanity not stop here, but take one noble step forward, and when she knocks off the convict's fetters, and lands him on the opposite shore, let her not turn her back and leave him there as if her duty were done; but let her *there* erect a noble institution where he can find a *kind* welcome and *instant* employment; before temptation, joining hands with his necessities, plunge him again headlong into the gulf of sin.

And here seems to me to be the loose screw in these institutions; admirably managed as many of them are, according to the prevalent ideas on the subject. You may tell me that I am a woman, and know nothing about it; and I tell you that I *want* to know. I tell you, that I don't believe the way to restore a man's lost self-respect is to degrade him before his fellow-creatures; to brand him, and chain him, and poke him up to show his points, like a hyena in a menagerie. No wonder that he growls at you, and grows vicious; no wonder that he eats the food you thrust between the bars of his cage with gnashing teeth, and a vow to take it out of the world somehow, when he gets out; no wonder that he thinks the Bible you place in his cell a humbug, and God a myth. I would have you startle up his self-respect by placing him in a position to show that you trusted him; I would have you give him something to hold in charge, for which he is in honor responsible; appeal to his *better* feelings, or if they smoulder almost to extinction, fan them into a flame for him out of that remnant of God's image which the vilest can never wholly destroy. *Anything but shutting a man up with hell in his heart to make him good.* The devils may well chuckle at it. And above all, tear down that taunting inscription over the prison-hall door at Blackwell's Island—"The way of transgressors is hard"—and place instead of it, "Neither do I condemn thee; go and sin no more."

Now, you can step aside, Mrs. Grundy; what I am about to write is not for your over-fastidious ear. *You,* who take by the hand the polished *roué,* and welcome him with a sweet smile to the parlor where sit your young, trusting daughters; you, who "have no business with his private life, so long as his manners are gentlemanly;" you who, while saying this, turn away with bitter, unwomanly words from his penitent, writhing victim. I ask no leave of *you* to speak of the wretched girls picked out of the gutters of New York streets, to inhabit those cells at Blackwell's Island. I speak not to *you* of what was tugging at my heartstrings as I saw them, that beautiful summer afternoon, file in, two by two, to their meals, followed by a man carrying a cowhide in his hand, by way of reminder; all this would not interest you; but when you tell me that these women are not to be named to ears polite, that our sons and our daughters should grow up ignorant of their existence, I stop my ears. As if they could, or did! As if they can take a step in the public streets without being jostled or addressed by them, or pained by their passing ribaldry; as if they could return from a party or concert at night, without meeting droves of them; as if they could, even in broad daylight, sit down to an ice-cream without having one for a *vis-à-vis.* As if they could ride in a car or omnibus, or cross in a ferry-boat, or go to a watering-place, without being unmistakably confronted by them. No, Mrs. Grundy; you know all this as well as I do. You would push them "anywhere out of the world," as unfit to live, as unfit to die; *they,* the weaker party, while their partners in sin, for whom you claim greater mental superiority, and who, by your own finding, should be much better able to learn and *to teach* the lesson of self-control—to them you extend perfect absolution. Most consistent Mrs. Grundy, get out of my way while I say what I was going to, without fear or favor of yours.

If I believed, as legislators, and others with whom I have talked on this subject, pretend to believe, they best know why, that God ever made one of those girls for the life they lead, for this in plain Saxon is what their talk amounts to, I should curse Him. If I could temporize as they do about it, as a "necessary evil," and "always has been, and always will be," and (then add this beautiful tribute to manhood) "that pure women would not be safe were it not so"—and all the other budget of excuses which this sin makes to cover its deformity—I would forswear my manhood.

You say their intellects are small, they are mere animals, naturally coarse and grovelling, Answer me this—are they, or are they not *immortal?* Decide the question whether *this* life is to be *all* to them. Decide before you shoulder the responsibility of such a girl's future. Granted she has only *this* life. God knows how much misery may be crowded into that. But you say, " Bless your soul, why do you talk to *me?* I have nothing to do with it; I am as virtuous as St. Paul." St. Paul was a bachelor, and of course is not my favorite apostle ; but waiving that, I answer, you *have* something to do with it when you talk thus, and throw your influence on the wrong side. No matter how outwardly correct your past life may have been, if you *really believe* what you say, I would not give a fig for your virtue if temptation and opportunity favored ; and if you talk so for talk's sake, and do not believe it, you had better " tarry at Jericho till your beard be grown."

But you say to me, "Oh, you don't know anything about it; men are differently constituted from women; woman's sphere is home." That don't suspend the laws of her being. That don't make it that she don't need sympathy and appreciation. That don't make it that she is never weary and needs amusement to restore her. Fudge. I believe in no difference that makes this distinction. Women lead, most of them, lives of unbroken monotony, and have much more need of exhilarating influences than men, whose life is out of doors in the breathing, active world. Don't tell me of shoemakers at their lasts, and tailors at their needles. Do either ever have to lay down their customers' coats and shoes fifty times a day, and wonder when the day is over why their work is *not* done, though they have struggled through fire and water to finish it? Do not both tailor and shoemaker have at least the variation of a walk to or from the shop to their meals? Do not their customers talk their beloved politics to them while they stitch, and do not their " confrères" run for a bottle of ale and crack merry jokes with them as their work progresses? Sirs! if monotony is to be avoided in man's life as injurious, if " variety" and exhilaration must always be the spice to his pursuits, how much more must it be necessary to a sensitively organized woman? If home is not sufficient (and I will persist that any *industrious, virtuous, unambitious* man, may have a home if he chooses); if home is not sufficient for him, why should it suffice for her? whose work is never done—who can have literally *no* such thing as system (and here's where a mother's discouragement comes in), while her babes are in their infancy; who often says to herself at night, though she would not for worlds part with one of them, "I can't tell what I have accomplished to-day, and yet I have not been idle a minute;" and day after day passes on in this way, and perhaps for weeks she does not pass the threshold for a breath of air, and yet men talk of "monotony!" and being "differently constituted," and needing amusement and exhilaration; and "business" is the broad mantle which it is not always safe for a wife to lift. I have no faith in putting women in a pound, that men may trample down the clover in a forty-acre lot. But enough for that transparent excuse.

The great Law-giver made no distinction of sex, as far as I can find out, when he promulgated the seventh commandment, nor should we. You tell me "society makes a difference;" more shame to it—more shame to the women who help to perpetuate it. You tell me that infidelity on the wife's part involves an unjust claim upon the husband and provider; and I ask you, on the other hand, if a good and virtuous wife has not a right to expect *healthy* children?

Let both be equally pure; let every man look upon every woman, whatsoever her rank or condition, as a sister whom his manhood is bound to protect, even, if need be, against herself, and let every woman turn the cold shoulder to any man of her acquaintance, how polished soever he may be, who would degrade her sex. Then this vexed question would be settled; there would be no such libels upon womanhood as I saw at Blackwell's Island, driven in droves to their cells. No more human traffic in those gilded palaces, which our children must not hear mentioned, forsooth! though their very fathers may help to support them, and which our tender-hearted legislators " can't see their way clear about." Then our beautiful rivers would no longer toss upon our island shores the "dead bodies of unfortunate young females."

SHALL WE HAVE MALE OR FEMALE CLERKS?

THE question whether male or female clerks in stores are preferred by shopping ladies, has lately been agitated. I do not hesitate to say that the majority of ladies would much prefer the former.

There are reasons for this, apart from the natural and obvious preference which women entertain for a coat and vest, before a chignon and panier. Male clerks, as a general thing, confine their attention to business; in other words, "mind what they are about." Female clerks are too often taking an inventory of the way you dress your hair; of the cut and trimming, and probable cost of your sacque and dress. No lady who shops much can be unaware of the coroner's inquest, favorable or otherwise, thus held over the dry-goods on her back. When you add to this the momentous computations, whether her jewelry is bogus or real, and where she got that love of a bonnet, there is grave room for fear lest by mistake she should roll you up two yards of ribbon instead of three, involving a journey back, to the disgust of yourself and your dress-maker; or, worse still, if the day be stormy, oblige you to coax your *dear* Charles to let you pin a sample on the lappel of his coat, and beg him just to stop a minute—there's a dear fellow—as he comes up town, and bring it to you. Of course, he gets talking with Tom Jones on politics, and forgets all about it, and only ejaculates, "pshaw!" when your horror-stricken dress-maker asks you for it.

That's how it is, although I get my ears boxed for saying it.

Mind you, I don't say that it is *always* so, no more than it is true that all male clerks attend strictly to the business in hand. Still it is true: that is really the fly in the ointment. In the words of the little hymn,

"It is their nature to."

Women *always* dissect each other the moment they meet, and never leave so much as a hair-pin unmeasured. So, as you can't change their nature, and as the instances are rare in which man, or woman either, can do two things correctly at the same moment, what are you going to do about it?

Having said this much, I am happy to add that I have favorite stores for shopping, where I am served by *female* clerks with a promptness, a politeness, an exactness and a dispatch, not to be exceeded by the best-trained *male* clerk in existence.

As to the silly girls and women who go shopping "for fun," and to make eyes, and chatter with clerks, there is no question how *their* preferences go on this question. We don't count their votes.

For myself, as my time is always limited, I desire *despatch*, first and foremost, with an exactness involving no *postscript* to my shopping; and I would also prefer female clerks, if I could include this. In fact I am willing, *in any case*, to give my vote for the female clerks, so much do I desire that my own sex should be helped to help themselves.

FASHIONABLE DISEASE.—The day when it was considered interesting and lady-like to be always ailing has gone by. Good health, fortunately, is the fashion. A rosy cheek is no longer considered "vulgar," and a fair, shapely allowance of flesh on the bones is considered the "style." Perhaps the great secret that good looks cannot exist without good health, may have had something to do with the care now taken to obtain it; whether this be so or not, future generations are the gainers all the same. A languid eye and a waxy, bloodless complexion, may go begging now for admiration. The "elegant stoop" in the shoulders, formerly considered so aristocratic, has also miraculously disappeared. Women walk more and ride less; they have rainy-day suits of apparel, too, which superfluity never was known to exist aforetime, sunshine being the only atmosphere in which the human butterfly was supposed to float. In short, "the fragile women of America" will soon exist only in the acid journal of some English traveller, who will, of course, stick to the by-gone fact as a still present reality, with a dogged pertinacity known only to that amiable nation.

UNKNOWN ACQUAINTANCES.

YOU have none? Then I am sorry for you. Much of my pleasure in my daily walks is due to them. Perhaps you go over the ground mechanically, with only dinner or business in your eye when you shall reach your journey's end. Perhaps you "don't see a soul," as you express it. Perhaps you have no "soul" yourself; only a body, of which you are very conscious, and whose claims upon you outweigh every other consideration. That is a pity. I wouldn't go round that treadmill for all the mines of Golconda. It always makes me think of that melancholy old horse one sees, pawing rotatory wood, at the way stations, on the railroad tracks; and because the sight makes every bone in me ache, my particular window-seat in the car is always sure to command a view of him. Now, come what will, I'll not be that horse. *You* may if you like, and I will cling to my dreams. I sha'n't live in this world forever, and I won't hurry over the ground and never see a sweet face as it flits past me, or a grand one, or a sorrowful one. I won't be deaf to the rippling laugh of a little child or the musical voice of a refined woman. It may be only two words that she shall speak, but they shall have a pleasant significance for me. Then there are strange faces I meet every day which I hope to keep on meeting till I die. Who was such an idiot as to say that "no woman ever sees beauty in another"? I meet every day a face that no man living could admire more than myself; soulful as well as beautiful. Lovely blue, pensive eyes; golden hair, waving over a pure white forehead; cheeks like the heart of a "blush rose;" and a grieved little rosy mouth, like that of a baby to whom for the first time you deny something, fearing lest it grow too wilful. I think that day lost in which I do not meet that sweet face, framed in its close mourning bonnet. Were I a man it is to that face I should immediately "make love."

Make love? Alas! I did not think how terribly significant was this modern term when I used it. Let no man *make* love to that face. But if there *is* one who *can* be in dead earnest, and *stay so*, I give my consent, provided he will not attempt to change the expression of that mouth.

I have another acquaintance. I don't care to ask "Who *is* that man?" I know that he has *lived* his life and not slept it away. I know that it has been a pure and a good one. It is written in his bright, clear, unclouded eye; in his springing step; in the smile of content upon his lip; in the lift of his shoulders; in the poise of his head; in the free, glad look with which he breathes in his share of the warm sunshine. Were he taken to the bedside of a sick man, it seems to me the very sight of him were health.

I used to have many unknown acquaintances among the little children in the parks; but what with French nurses and silk velvet coats, I have learned to turn my feet elsewhere. It gives me the heart-ache to see a child slapped for picking up a bright autumn leaf, though it *may* chance to be "dirty;" or denied a smooth, round pebble, on account of a dainty little glove that must be kept immaculate. I get out of temper, and want to call on all their mothers and fight Quixotic battles for the poor little things, as if it would do any good; as if mothers who dress their children that way to play, cared for anything *but* their looks.

Then I have some unknown acquaintances in the yard of a large house in the upper part of Broadway. I never asked who lived in the house; but I thank him for the rare birds of brilliant plumage who walk to and fro in it, or perch upon the window-sills or steps, as proudly conscious of their gay feathers as the belles who rustle past. I love to imagine the beautiful countries they came from, and the flowers that blossomed there, and the soft skies that arched over them. I love to see them pick up their food so daintily, and, with head on one side, eye their many admirers looking through the fence, as if to say—beat *that* if you can in America! Ah! my birdies, stop your crowing; just wait a bit and see how the "*American Eagle*" is going to come out, and how each time they who have tried to clip his wings have only found that it made them grow broader and stronger. Soft skies and sweet flowers are very nice things, birdies; but rough winds and freedom are better for the soul.

I have said nothing of unknown acquaintances among my favorite authors. How many times—did I not so hate the sight of a pen when "school is let out"—have I longed to express to them my love and gratitude. Nor, judging by myself, could I ever say, "they do not need it;" since there are, or should be, moments in the experience of all writers when they regard with a dissatisfied eye what they have already given to the world, when sympathetic, appreciative words, warm from the heart, are hope and inspiration to the receiver.

A LINK BETWEEN HUSBANDS AND WIVES.—Blessed be the little children who make up so unconsciously our life-disappointments. How many couples, mutually unable to bear each other's faults, or to forbear the causes of irritation, find solace for their pain in these golden links which still continue to unite them. On that they are one. *There* they can really repose. Those fragile props keep them from quite sinking disheartened by life's roadside. How often has a little hand drawn amicably together two else-unwilling ones, and made them see how bright and blessed earth may become in pronouncing that little word—"forgive."

LIFE AND ITS MYSTERIES.

WAS there ever a romance in that man or that woman's life? I *used* to ask myself, as I looked upon a hard face which stoicism seemed to have frozen over, through the long years. Was there ever a moment when, for that man, or woman, love transfigured everything, or the want of it threw over the wide earth the pall of unrest? Have they ever wept, or laughed, or sighed, or clasped hands in passionate joy or sorrow? *Had* they any life? Or have they simply vegetated like animals? Did they see any beauty in rock, mountain, sky, or river, or was this green earth a browsing place, nothing more?

I never ask those questions now; for I know how much fire may be hidden under a lava-crusted exterior. I know that though the treasure-chest *may* sometimes be locked when it is empty, oftener beneath the fastening lies the wealth, which the right touch can at any moment set free. There are divers masks worn in this harlequin world of ours. Years ago I met, in travelling, a lady who seemed to me the very embodiment of fun and frolic. Like a humming-bird, she never was still; alighting now here, now there, wheresoever were sunshine, sweetness and perfume. One day, as we were rambling in the woods, we sat down to rest under a tree, after our frolicking. Some little word of mine, as I drew her head into my lap, and smoothed the hair on her temples, transformed her. With a sharp, quick cry of agony, she threw her arms about my neck, weeping as I never saw a woman weep. When she was quiet came the sad story. The trouble battled with, and bravely borne. The short, joyous years—then the long days, and nights, and weeks, and months, so full of desolation and bitterness, and life yet at its meridian. How should she meet the long, slow-moving years? That was the question she asked me. "Tell me how! you who know—tell me how!"

And this was the woman I thought frivolous and pleasure-seeking. Wearing beneath that robe the penitential cross, reminding her at every moment with its sharp twinge of pain, that try as she might, she could never fly from herself.

How often, when I have been inclined to judge harshly, have I thought of that Gethsemane cry. It is sorrowful how we misjudge each other in this busy world. How very near we may be to a warm heart, and yet be frozen! How carelessly we pass by the pool of Bethesda, with its waiting crowd, without thinking that we might be the angel to trouble the waters? This thought is often oppressive to me in the crowd of a city hurrying home at nightfall. What burden does this man or that woman carry, known only to their Maker? How many among them may be just at the dividing line between hope and despair! And how some faces remind you of a dumb animal, who bears its pain meekly and mournfully, yet cringing lest some careless foot should, at any moment, render it unendurable; haunting you as you go to your home as if you were verily guilty in ignoring it.

Have you never felt this? and, although you may have been cheated and imposed upon seventy times seven, can you wholly stifle it? and *ought* you to try, even though you know how well the devil can wear the livery of heaven?

I think it is this that, to the reflecting and observing, makes soul and body wear out so quickly in the city. These constantly recurring, unsolvable problems, which cloud faith and make life terrible, instead of peaceful and sweet; which lead us sometimes to look upon the little child, so dear to us, with such cowardly fear, that it would be a relief to lay it, then and there, in the arms of the Good Shepherd, lest *it*, too, stray away from the fold.

SWEARERS AND SWEARING.—Profanity is such a *cheap* accomplishment! "Damme!" "Damn it!" The idea that "*gentlemen*," so called, should use these expletives, in which the commonest laborer, who can scarcely "make his mark" to a document, can excel him! As a matter of taste, setting aside any question of morality, the practice of it by "cultivated persons" is our daily wonder.

MRS. WASHINGTON'S ETERNAL KNITTING.

THERE are many-sided men and women, and there are men and women that are one-sided, both in brains and body. There are men of business who have no surplus left after attending to their business. There are women who have no surplus left after attending to their kettles and pans and their mending basket. On the other hand, there are men whom business does not wholly absorb; who are interested intelligently, and actively, too, in every great question of the day and hour. There are women who order their houses discreetly, tastefully, and economically, and can yet converse elegantly and with knowledge with the most cultured persons of both sexes.

This is a preface to some little remarks of mine on an article lately written by a gentleman in one of our Magazines, on the wife of General (Cherry-Tree) Washington.

This writer says that Mrs. Washington's "knitting was never out of her hands; that when callers came, the click of her needles was always an accompaniment to her conversation. That she deemed it a privilege to attend to the details of housekeeping, and regarded the days when her official position required her presence in the drawing-room as *lost.*"

Now she is a specimen of what I should call a one-sided woman. I am glad she was an accomplished housekeeper, and better still, was not above attending to her duty there. It was splendid, in her high position, that she should set so good an example in this regard. But it was *not* good to keep her needles clicking when callers came, as if to say, You are an intruder, and I can ill endure your presence. This, I maintain, was neither necessary nor polite. It was *not* good that she could consider her "drawing-room days" as lost, and not perceive that they might be turned to account in elevating, as an intelligent woman can, the tone of the society she moved in. That she took the contrary view of it shows, to my thinking, that she was *not* truly an intelligent woman. I believe her duty, as the wife of an American President, lay there quite as much as in looking over her household economies. But that was *Then,* and this is *Now!* In those days one-sided men and women were plenty, and many-sided men and women rare. We can point to-day to many glorious examples of the latter, thank Heaven.

It was once considered a disgrace to a woman to know enough to spell correctly; and if, in addition to committing this indiscretion, she happened to disgrace herself by a knowledge of French or Latin, let her never speak of it, lest it should "destroy her chances of marriage." The idea is losing ground that a woman's mentality perils puddings and shirt-buttons. There have been too many shining, tasteful houses and well-ordered tables presided over by cultivated women, for any man nowadays to drag up that old fogyism, without raising a laugh for himself.

When I read this article about Mrs. Washington, who, I admit, was excellent as far as she went, I called the writer to an account. He replied, "Oh, I knew you'd pitch into me, Fanny;" and not liking to disappoint him, I have.

RELIGIOUS TOLERANCE.—It would do no harm if Christians who are disposed to judge harshly of each other, were to read occasionally the accounts handed down to us of enormities committed some centuries ago, and even in later years, in the name of religion, upon those of differing creeds; the perpetrators sincerely believing at the time that they were doing God service. When we are tempted to shut the gate of heaven in any fellow-mortal's face, let us recall these things, at which humanity and Christianity should alike shudder. Said a good old man, in dying, of a son who had embraced another faith than that taught him, "Well, it matters not by which road John gets to heaven, if he only reaches it at last." It seems to us that this, taken rightly, is the true spirit.

THE WOMAN QUESTION.

I HAVE been sitting here, enjoying a quiet laugh all by myself, over a pile of newspapers and magazines, in which the "Woman Question" was aired according to the differing views of editors and writers. One gentleman thinks that the reason the men take a nap on the sofa, evenings at home, or else leave it to go to naughty places, is because there are no Madame De Staëls in our midst to make home attractive. He was probably a bachelor, or he would understand that when a man who has been perplexed and fretted all day, finally reaches home, the last object he wishes to encounter is a wide-awake woman of the Madame De Staël pattern, propounding her theories on politics, theology, and literature. The veriest idiot who should entertain him by the hour with tragic accounts of broken tea-cups and saucepans, would be a blessing compared to her; not that he would like that either; not that he would know himself exactly what he *would* like in such a case, except that it should be something diametrically opposite to that which years ago he got on his knees to solicit.

Another writer asserts that women's brains are too highly cultivated at the present day; and that they have lost their interest in the increase of the census; and that their husbands, not sharing their apathy, hence the disastrous result. I might suggest in answer that this apathy may have its foundation in the idea so fast gaining ground—thanks to club-life, and that which answers to it in a less fashionable strata of society—that it is an indignity to expect fathers of families to be at home, save occasionally to sleep, or eat, or to change their apparel; and that, under such circumstances, women naturally prefer to be the mother of four children, or none, than to engineer seventeen or twenty through the perils of childhood and youth without assistance, co-operation, or sympathy.

Another writer thinks that women don't "smile" enough when their husbands come into the house; and that many a man misses having his shirt or drawers taken from the bureau and laid on a chair all ready to jump into at some particular day or hour, as he was accustomed when he lived with some pattern sister or immaculate aunt at home. This preys on his manly intellect, and makes life the curse it is to him.

Another asserts that many women have some female friend who is very objectionable to the husband, in exerting a pugilistic effect on her mind, and that he flees his house in consequence of this unholy influence; not that this very husband wouldn't bristle all over at the idea of his wife's court-martialing a bachelor or benedict friend, for the same reason; but then it makes a difference, you know, a man not being a woman.

Another writer asserts that nobody yet knows what woman is capable of doing. I have only to reply that the same assertion cannot be made with regard to men, as the dwellers in great cities, at least, know that the majority of them are capable of doing anything that the devil and opportunity favor.

It has been a practice for years to father every stupid joke that travels the newspaper-round on "*Paddy*"—poor "Paddy." In the same way it seems to me that for every married man now, who proves untrue to his better nature, *his wife* is to be held responsible. It is the old cowardly excuse that the first man alive set going, and which has been travelling round this weary world ever since. "The woman thou gavest to be with me"—*she* did thus and so; and therefore all the Adams from that time down have whimpered, torn their hair, and rushed forth to the long-coveted perdition, over the bridge of this cowardly excuse.

One of the sapient advisers of women ridicules the idea of a woman's voting till she has learned to be "moderate" in following the fashions; moderate in her household expenses; moderate in her way of dressing her hair; moderate in the length of her party-robes and in the shortness of her walking costume. Till woman has attained this desirable moderation he declares her totally unfit for the ballot.

Granted—for the sake of the argument, granted; but as it is a poor rule that won't work both ways, suppose we determine a man's fitness for the ballot by the same rule. Let not his short-tailed coats refuse to be sat upon by the fat owner thereof. Let not his pantaloons be so tight that he cannot stoop without danger. Let not his overcoat flap against his heels, because a new-fangled custom demands an extra inch or two. Let not the crown of his hat pierce the skies, or be so ridiculously shallow as to convey the idea that it belongs to his little son. Let him smoke "moderately." Let him drink "moderately." Let him drive "moderately." Let him stock-gamble "moderately." Let him stay out at night "moderately." Let him, in short, prepare himself by a severe training in the virtue of "moderation" for the privilege of casting a vote.

Why, there is not a man in the land who wouldn't sniff at the idea! and yet I suppppose it never occurred to the writer of this advice to women that he was uttering impertinent nonsense, or that the rules he laid down were quite as well suited to his own sex as to ours.

Every day I see gentlemen who are as much walking advertisements of their tailor's last exaggerated fashion as any foolish woman could be of her dressmaker's newly fledgéd insanity. If Bismarck be the rage, or Metternich green, their neckties and gloves slavishly follow Fashion's behest. Hats, coats, trousers are long-tail or short, tight or loose, as she bids; and that whether legs are straight or crooked, whether the outline is round or angular, whether the owner looks like an interrogation-point, or a tub on two legs. At least he is in the fashion—that manly thought consoles him.

If "moderation" in smoking were the test of fitness for the ballot-box, how many men do you think would be able to vote?

Oh, pshaw! Advice to women will go in at one ear and out at the other, while male advisers are such egregious fools. The silliest woman who ever cleaned the streets with her silken robe, or exhibited thick ankles in a short one, or froze her ears in January in a saucer of a bonnet, knows that she can find a parallel for all her nonsense in the male side of the question. Men inhabit too many glass-houses for them at present to hurl missiles of that sort at their fair neighbors. Reform *yourselves*, gentlemen. *You* who are so much mightier and stronger and more competent, by *your own showing*, show us, poor, weak, "grown-up children" how to behave pretty!

A Word for the Little Ones.—Have one rough suit for your little ones, this summer, to tumble about the dirt in. The amount of happiness they will get out of that rough suit, and their liberty in it, is not to be computed by any parent's arithmetic. Only a child brought up to city pavements and fine clothes can add up that sum. Will you do it, mothers? Just for this one summer, if no more. Leave off for a time the sashes and laces, and let the little ones get happily, and, what is better, *healthily* dirty.

TWO KINDS OF WIVES.

SOME writer remarks, "We blunder fearfully with our domesticity in America. Our wives are only of two kinds: the family slave on one hand; the frivolous woman of fashion on the other!"

"*Our* wives!" As a *woman* can't have a "wife," I may logically infer that a man wrote the above paragraph, though without these two helping words I should have come to the same conclusion. Now so far as my limited knowledge goes, we generally find "in the market" that which is oftenest called for. Put that down in your memorandum book, sir. Men are but just beginning to find out that the two specimens of womankind referred to are much more difficult to get along with, in the main, than a woman of intelligence and mentality. I say they are just *beginning* to understand it. Men are very fond of the results that the "family slave" brings about, in the shape of good food and well-mended clothes, but they dodge with a fox's cunning the creaking and jarring of the machinery by which these results are obtained. They never want to be on hand when any process of disentanglement is necessary that defies temporarily the "family slave." Just then "business" is imperative—very likely in the shape of a journey—till the household machine runs smoothly again; nor does he care to hear how it is done, so that he is not bothered about it. If the "family slave" gets thinner and thinner, why, it is because "she takes everything *so hard.*" She ought not to take things hard! That's her fault! It is an unfortunate nervousness which she ought to try to get rid of, because—it worries *him!* She is "no companion" for him—not a bit! When he wants to be amused, she is too tired to do it. In fact she don't see anything to be amused at. That is another unfortunate peculiarity of hers, this looking on the dark side of things. *He* don't do so. Not he! He deplores it; he sits down and writes just such a paragraph as I have just quoted above, like the consistent man he is.

I once heard a man who was in excellent circumstances, and whose young wife, just recovered from a severe illness, had taken her twelve-pound baby in her weak arms, and gone into the country for a few days, remark, as she left, "She *would* take all my old trousers with her to mend—God bless her!" adding, hallelujah-wise, "*There's a wife for you!*"

Now who made *that* "family slave"? Because she was magnanimous and self-forgetful, must he need be a brute? Women must take care of themselves in these matters. They must husband their strength for future demands, since their husbands won't husband it. That man was abundantly able to pay a tailor or a seamstress to repair his clothes.

Instead of contenting himself with God-blessing this little meek wife, he should, like a true man, have positively *forbidden* her to work at all, in this short reprieve from household care. When there is nothing left of her but one front tooth, and a back, bent like the letter C, he will contemplate some round, rosy woman, who has not yet met her doom, and wonder how his wife came " to lose all her good looks so soon."

As to " fashionable women," were there no fashionable men, I don't imagine that they would exist on this planet. " She is so dowdy!" " She is so stylish!" ' Do you suppose the women who hear these masculine comments forget them? And do you suppose when, to use an equine expression, you have once given a wife "her head," by your admiration of "style" and fashion, that you can rein her up short, whenever you take a notion? Don't she hear you sneering at intelligent women, and don't she see you flattering fashionable fools?

Of course she does. Now let every man ask himself, before he sits down to write against the faults and follies of women, what he, individually, has done to form and perpetuate them? And if ever, in his whole life, when he saw a woman wronging her better self in *any* way, he extended a manly, brotherly hand to her, in the endeavor to lead her right? or, if he did not, on the contrary, join her, and walk with her, *well pleased*, in her own ill-selected path.

UNDERTAKERS' SIGNS ON CHURCHES.

IT may strike *you* pleasantly, but when I am about to enter a church, the conspicuous intelligence upon its outside walls, that the "undertaker may be found at such a street," is anything but a pleasant announcement. Now not being myself a theologian of that school which compels a smiling countenance to be left at the *porch* of the "meetin'-house," I can, therefore, by no means indorse any gloomy surroundings, outside or inside.

One of the principal articles of *my* creed is, that Sunday should be the pleasantest day of all the week. When I open my eyes to its dawn, I always rejoice, if instead of a gray, cloudy sky, it be a lovely blue, and the sun be shining brightly; I think upon the thousands to whom this day is the only leisure day of all the seven; the thousands who, without this blessed rest, would scarcely have time to look upon the faces of wife or children; scarcely time to receive the regenerating caresses of little twining arms, or hear the recital of little griefs and joys which it is so blessed to share with one who never wearies in the hearing, and to whose fatherly ear nothing a little child can say is "trifling." It is blessed to me to think of the thousand humble homes where the Sabbath sun shines upon just such a scene as this; preaching *through the family* this simple gospel: that the humblest have those for whom they must strive to leave the legacy of a good and honest name. Now when a working-man, with his heart full of love and happiness, walks forth on a Sunday morning, do you think it wise when he approaches a church to shake a coffin in his face? Had I my way, I would tear these undertaker-placards all down to-morrow, and instead, I would write this, "Strangers furnished with free seats here every Sunday." Were I a clergyman, an undertaker should no more use my church walls to advertise his business, than the upholsterer who furnished the pew-cushions, or the bookseller who provided the hymn-books, or the man who found the gas-fixtures. Ah! but you say it is very convenient to know where the sexton lives. Very well, so it is; but let him advertise in the papers, as other people do, who have no convenient church walls to save their advertising fees. The truth is, that the whole undertaker business, as at present managed, is monstrously mis-managed. The other day, in one of our streets, I saw an oyster shop with heaps of bivalves curiously arranged in the window, over which was written: "*Live and let live.*" Next door, being an undertaker, he had piled ostentatiously *his* wares, consisting of heaps of "fancy coffins," in his show-window. If he had only copied his bivalve-neighbor, so far as to write over the window, *Die and let die*, the farce would have been complete.

They who please may sniff at Sunday. To us it is a blessed reprieve from care and business, and worry of every sort. The very putting on of the fresh, clean, "best" raiment, is suggestive of best thoughts and best feelings for all whom we meet, and more than all, for the dear ones at home, whose happiness it is ours to make or to mar. Then the sweet, soothing hymn and the pleading prayer; and the sermon, in which it were hard, as a rule, to find nothing that we could not take home with us for our improvement and self-help. Then the pleasant family group at table, where the children *should* be. Ah! *we* are glad for this blessed Sunday, let him who will, decry or pervert it.

A PITIABLE SIGHT.—There is no more pitiable sight than that of a husband and father reeling home at the end of the week, having left the greater part of his week's wages at some drinking saloon. We think of the patient, toiling wife and hungry children, and the miserable Sunday, and the coming week in store for them, and the utter hopelessness of their future lot, and can find no words of denunciation strong enough for the man who grows rich by tempting a brother's weakness, knowing, when he does so, that for his victim there is in this world no redemption.

A VOICE FROM THE SKATING POND.

COATS and trousers have the best of it *everywhere*, I exclaimed, for the thousandth time, as I looked at the delightful spectacle of the male and female skaters at the Central Park. Away went coat and trousers, like a feather before the wind; free, and untrammelled by dry-goods, and independent of any chance somerset; while the poor, skirt-hampered women glided circumspectly after their much-needed health and robustness, with that awful omnipresent sense of *the proprieties,* (and—horror of horrors—a tumble!) which sends more of the dress-fettered sex to their graves every year than any disease *I* wot of. That a few women whom I saw there had had the perseverance to become tolerable skaters, with all that mass of drygoods strung round their waists, is infinitely to their credit. How much *longer* and better they could have skated, disembarrassed, as men are, of these swaddling robes, common sense will tell anybody. I should like to see how long a *man's* patience would hold out, floundering round in them, while *he* learned to skate! And yet were a lady to adopt any other costume, how decent soever, or how eminently soever befitting the occasion, what a rolling of eyes and pursing of mouths should we see from the strainers at gnats and swallowers of camels. All these thoughts passed through my mind as I mixed in with the merry crowd on that bracing winter day, whose keen breath was like rare old wine, so did it stir and warm the blood; and I wondered, as I gazed at those dress-fettered women, whether those heathen nations who strangled their female babies at birth were as naughty as we had been told they were!

"Why don't *you* get up a skating costume, Fanny, and set them an example?" whispers a voice at my elbow. *Me?* why don't *I?* Because, sir, custom has made me a poor, miserable coward in these matters, like the rest of my sex, and because, moreover, sir, you would have no more courage to walk by my side in such a costume, than I should have to wear it. No, no: a crowd of curious men in my wake would be no more agreeable in reality than it is in perspective. It is brave *talking*, I know, but the time has not yet come when men, by refraining from rude remarks on a female pioneer in such a cause, would remove one of the chief obstacles to its advancement. They "like healthy women"—oh, of course they do! but then, unfortunately, they like dainty prettiness of attire much better. Else, why don't they encourage women when they try to do a sensible thing? Why do they grin, and stroke their beards, and shrug their shoulders, and raise their eyebrows, and go home to Jane Maria, and say, "Let me catch *you* out in such a costume"? Till all that is done away with, we must be content to see puny, waxy-looking children, and read in "Notes on America" the usual number of stereotyped pages on "the fragility of our women." Now, let me say in closing that I don't wish to be misunderstood on this matter. I approve of no costume which a delicate-minded, self-respecting, dignified woman might not wear in public. But I will insist that nothing *can* be done in the way of reform, while husbands and fathers and brothers *sniff* the whole subject "under the table" as soon as it is mentioned. May every one of them have a yearly doctor's bill to pay as long as the moral law!

BEARING TROUBLE.—There are persons who emerge from every affliction and trouble and vexation, purified like fine gold from out the furnace. There are others, and they are the more numerous, who are imbittered and soured, and made despondent and apathetic. We think the latter belong to the class who *try to stand alone* during these storms of life, instead of looking above for aid. When one can truly say, "He doeth all things well," the sting is taken out of affliction, the tears are dried, and the courage given to bear what the future has in store. This, we think, makes the great difference between these two classes.

THE SIN OF BEING SICK.

I WISH women could be made to understand the importance of flannel under-clothing, and warm outer-clothing, and common-sense generally in food and exercise, when they talk about longing to have a "profession" or a "career." Not that good health should not always be a sort of religion with them; but they should remember that what failings soever men may have, as a general thing they are not such fools as to shiver in insufficient clothing when other may be had, or to go with wet or cold feet, because thick stockings "fill up the boot," or reject thick-soled boots because they make the feet look a size or two larger. They do not, either, think it attractive to bare their throats and necks to a biting wind in the street, thus inviting a blue nose and the pitying contempt of every beholder. Woman's great foe, "headache," is surely invited and perpetuated by these follies, even if no worse punishment follows. "I am so shivery all over!" you will hear these silly creatures exclaim, and the red and white located in the wrong spots in their faces attest the truth of it. One would think that, as a matter upon which their much-valued good looks depend, they would "consider their ways, and be wise;" but no. After this they come in and call for some "hot, strong tea." Tea! *that woman's dram!* morning, noon, and night. It makes her "feel like another being," she says. I'm sure it makes her *act* like one. This lasts an hour, perhaps; then she has such a "gnawing at her stomach." Then follows depression after the exhilaration. Then she eats nothing, because she has "no appetite." Then—another cup of tea, to " set her up," as she calls it.

I should like to see such a woman having any "career," except fitting herself speedily for a lunatic asylum. Such a course is reprehensible and suicidal enough, when good food is at hand and enough of it, and the women who practise it have money enough to pay a doctor to come and see them, and tell them lies, and give them nice messes to make believe cure them. But unfortunately our working girls and women, who have only a hospital bed to look forward to when sick, go on after the same crazy fashion. There is some shadow of excuse with them for their intemperate use of *tea;* the horrible fare of their boarding-places being so unpalatable and disgusting, and their long hours of labor so exhaustive and discouraging that this stimulant has become *seemingly* necessary to their existence—the one bit of comfort and luxury that they look forward to with eagerness in the interval of work. "I can't do without it," said a young shop-girl to me, when I remonstrated with her on its use, morning, noon, and night. "I couldn't do my work without it." And how did she spend the wages received for "her work"? In a flimsy, showy dress; in a gay hat; in a fashionable pair of boots with high heels. Meantime she had no flannel; she had no *thick* boots; she had no warm outer garments; she had nothing to insure either health or comfort, and she was in the same alternatives of exhilaration and depression as her richer sisters of whom I have spoken. I don't know why, either, that I should call them "richer," except that *they* could have a rosewood coffin with silver nails, and be buried in a fashionable cemetery, while the working-girl would have a pine one, and sleep her long sleep in the Potter's Field. Oh, dear! I see all these abuses, and I exclaim, Oh, the rare and priceless blessings of good health and common-sense! How I wish that every clergyman in our land—only that I know that in many cases they are as great sinners themselves in the matter of health—would preach on the *sin of being sick*.

Now *there's* a topic for those of them who have the face to speak of it, and a clear conscience to bear them out in it. For those of them who don't sit in their libraries smoking till you can't see across it, when they should be knocking about in the open air, cultivating a breezy, sunny, healthful state of mind and body—just the same as if they were laymen, instead of "ministers," whom the devil desires, of all things, to see solemn and dyspeptic.

I lately read an article in one of our papers headed, "*Have we a Healthy Woman among us?*"

I fully indorse what the writer says as to the marvellous amount of invalidism among our girls and women, and I deplore it as sincerely as he does. But let us have fair play on this subject. If there are few of them who ever ought to be wives and mothers, I ask, how much better qualified—physiologically speaking—are the young *men* of the present day to be husbands and fathers? Go to any physician of large practice and experience, and if he answers you frankly and truthfully, you will learn that it is six of one and half a dozen of the other. When boys of eight and twelve go to school with a satchel in one hand and a cigar in the other, I wouldn't give much for their future vitality, even without leaving a margin for other violations of the laws of health. It would be well, while publicly deploring "tight lacing" and "tight shoes" for girls, privately to inquire about the practice of smoking for boys in short-jackets. To be sure, I cannot see with what face a father, who is himself a bond-slave to this habit, can ask his boy to refrain from doing that which he, as a man, has not had self-control enough to accomplish. But don't let him then write or speak dolefully about the miserable ill-health of our girls and women, not, at least, till he moves out of his own "glass-house." If the *truthful* inscriptions were placed upon the myriad little graves in our cemeteries, it would be *fathers*, not *mothers*, in many cases, who could not read them without pangs of remorse.

The day will, I hope, come, when the marriage

question will cease to be decided by Cupid or cupidity; when parents, and lovers, themselves, will consider a sound, healthy body to be of primary importance. Oh! the weary years of watching and dosing and misery for two, consequent upon the neglect of this precaution! Oh! the army of puny and idiotic children, doomed, if they live to adult years, to be a blight in themselves and to all around them! And how distressing is it to see a wife, made gloriously as a woman should be, with a broad chest, a free, firm, graceful step and a beaming face, married to a man whose only claim to be a living being is, that he has not yet ceased to breathe! And still as mournful is it, to look at a kingly man, whose very presence is so full of life that it is like stepping from a close room into the glad, free, balmy sunshine even to come where he is, married to a little pink-eyed, feeble dwarf of a creature, with little paws like a bird's, and not life enough left even to chirp to him.

"Well, what are you going to do about it?" as the pre-Raphaelite friend asked of a disconsolate widow who kept on crying for her dead husband.

That's just the point where I want to bring *you*, my reader. I want you individually to look first for good health in the chosen wife who is to be the mother of your children. And you, young girl, look first for that rarity, a *clean bill of health*, with your future husband. A brown-stone house and a carriage and livery are nothing to it. Take my advice. Don't take copper for gold on the health question, and *don't give it*.

ARE MINISTERS SERFS?

WE hear a great outcry occasionally about "ministers who work outside of their profession," as it is called—that is, in the lecture field, or in writing newspaper or magazine articles for pay, or in editing newspapers; and this although the ministers thus censured are faithful to their pastoral duties, and bring forth every Sunday, and during the week, fresh, vigorous thoughts for the profit and pleasure of these complainers.

Now in our view this is a great impertinence.

Suppose a clergyman has a decrepit mother or sister, whose only pecuniary reliance, is himself? Suppose he is not willing, from delicacy toward them, to turn his family affairs inside out, and explain *why* he does this "outside work," which may enable him to meet this or some similar outside demand? *Is it* properly anybody's business? If he do not defraud his parish, have they any right to hold a coroner's inquest over his "outside" earnings and their possible appropriation? How would his deacons or church-members stand such a scrutiny over their own private affairs? We think that the "old Adam" in them would soon rear and plunge at it. Well, ministers are men too, though you sometimes seem to forget it; and *they* don't like it either. The parish has not purchased their *souls*, as I understand it, no more than have husbands those of their wives. Let us hope, in this enlightened age, that neither are serfs. Let us hope that all ministers, and all wives too, all over the land, may honestly and innocently earn money, and keep it in a private purse too, without accounting to either the parish or their husbands for the expenditure of the same; or without, in either case, causing unfounded suspicion or breach of the peace, or officious meddling, no more, in my opinion, to be justified, than as if the "boot was on the other foot," where Mrs. Grundy would consider it a great wrong to place it, or to insist upon its being worn, regardless of the limping or contortions of the wearers.

Before either parishes or husbands complain of outside *honest* earnings, let them inquire if the salaries they give are just and ample. Let them both inquire whether the objection they have to outside earning in both cases, does not mainly arise from the fear that the curious public will imagine that they are not.

Of course, in saying all this, I am referring to those clergymen and those married women who are sensible and judicious, as well as blessed with ability, and it is my opinion that Mrs. Grundy has meddled long enough with the proper independence and self-respect of both.

One thing I've forgotten, namely, parishes are not to suppose that an increase of a clergyman's salary is to padlock his lips afterward, if he is requested, or if he feels inclined, to deliver his sentiments, even "for pay," on the platform, as well as in the pulpit they have called him to fill. Nor after that, are they to handcuff him either, lest he should write a line "for pay" in a paper or magazine? In short, do try to be willing that your "minister" should stand up straight like any other man, and not go cringing round the world a bought serf, with his "white choker" for a badge of the same. I'm sick of seeing it. If I were a minister, it would take all the religion I could muster to keep me from saying wicked words about it.

"Our minister was away six weeks this summer," said a person complainingly, the other day. Well, are not ministers human? Must they not eat, drink, rest, sleep, sorrow and grieve, like other mortals? Have they not, in addition to all this, a constant and exhaustive demand upon their sympathies for the griefs of other people? And must they not constantly be racking their brains, in and out of the pulpit, to have all their words set fitly, like "apples of gold in pictures of silver"? And is it not better that a minister should rest "six weeks" than be laid useless upon the shelf for six months, or that his voice should be silenced forever because of the exactions of the unthinking portion of his hearers? And would it not be well if the persons thus complaining spent the time instead in looking to it that they had profited by what they had *already* heard?

Whatever else you grudge, never grudge a good, faithful minister a breathing spell.

BLAMING PROVIDENCE FOR OUR OWN FAULTS.

NAPOLEON is said to have lost a battle on account of an underdone leg of mutton. Now, there are many who, shaking their heads, would say, it was "an overruling Providence." I have to smile sometimes at poor "Providence"—that convenient scapegoat for all the human stupidity extant;—who kills little babies, and puts a tombstone over young girls who should have lived to be the healthy mothers of healthy sons and daughters. This "All-wise Providence," who, as some would have us believe, is malignantly and perpetually employed in tripping up the heels of human beings for the benefit of the undertaker—what a convenient theology for bad cooks, for unwise school-teachers, for selfish, careless, ignorant parents!

Now "Providence" does no such things. Providence approves of live, fat, rollicking babies; of deep-chested women; of round, healthy girls; of muscular men; and sound physical specimens of every kind. Bless you—*he* don't bend spines, nor make drunkards, nor thieves, nor write a shameful history on the pure brow of any woman who ever has or ever shall live; *he* don't ordain perpendicular ghosts of ministers, to defile sepulchrally through creation, and scare people into heaven. *He* don't smile on those suicidal mothers, who run breathlessly round and round the nursery treadmill, thinking they are doing God service, till they drop dead in the harness, and leave eight or nine children motherless, at an age when they most need maternal guidance. *He* don't manufacture scrofulous constitutions out of unwholesome food, and bad ventilation, and dissipated habits. It is *not* one of the ten commandments that babies should be taught Greek and Latin before they have cut their teeth, that they may become idiots before maturity; or that schoolboys should smoke pipes and cigars; or that schoolgirls should drink strong coffee for breakfast, and eat rich pastry and pickles for luncheon. It is high time that people shouldered their own sins, and called things by their right names, and told the truth at funerals, and on tombstones, if they *must* say anything there. In my opinion, an "All-wise and inscrutable Providence" has borne quite blasphemy enough in this way.

A CHAPTER ON NURSES.

CAN anybody tell why nurses are fat? Is there anything in the atmosphere of a sick room, or in the sight of phials, pills, leeches, potions, blisters, and plasters to give one an appetite? I solemnly affirm that I never saw a bony nurse—never. There's a horrid mystery about it which I have in vain tried to solve. With what a lazy waddle they roll round the apartment, and how your flesh creeps as they fix their unsympathizing eyes upon you; you are so sure that they had just as lief bring you your shroud as a clean nightcap; that it is quite immaterial to them whether the next thing that comes through the door is a bowl of gruel or your coffin; in fact, that they would be immensely gratified if you'd hurry up your dying, and let them off to the pleasurable excitement of a new subject.

And then that professional sniffle when a visitor asks, "How is your patient, nurse?" It is a poor satisfaction, to make faces at her under the sheet, as she answers; but I have done it; I shouldn't be surprised now, if you thought that was unamiable. Ah! you never had her twitch down the curtain over a lovely sunset, that was soothing you like a cool hand on your forehead, and light a little, nasty "nurse-lamp," merely because she knew you hadn't strength enough to say, "Please don't." A nurse-lamp! that you have contemplated night after night in the silent, dreary watches, till it seemed like an evil eye, glimmering and glowing, fascinating you in spite of yourself, till the perspiration stood in cold drops on your forehead, while the watch went "tick," "tick," and the fat, old nurse snored away, and each nerve in your body seemed a separate and more perfect engine of torture. No wonder you hate to see her unnecessarily shorten the daylight and repeat the horror. But she'll do it; of course she'll do it. If you had not wanted her to, you should have told her that of all sublunary things, you fancied a night-lamp. Now I leave it to you, if, after that and kindred crucifixions of momentary occurrence, you could stand that pious sniffle with which she answers the question, "How is your patient, nurse?"

And then, if she wouldn't be so excruciatingly officious at such a time, one might swallow one's disgust. If, when a visitor comes in, she wouldn't twitch your pillow from under your head, just as you are knowing your first comfortable moment, and giving it a shake and a pat, thrust it under your head again, forcing your chin down into your breast-bone, and half dislocating your neck, just to show them how attentive she is; if she wouldn't strip down the blanket, or pile on a dozen quilts, when you are just the right temperature, for the same reason, I think it would be more jolly. Then if, after all that, she wouldn't stand, and *keep* standing, so near the corner of your mouth, that you couldn't call her some "rantankerous" name by way of relief; though, at another time, when you were dying for a glass of water, she'd leave you all alone and take half an hour to get it; if she wouldn't do all these things; but she will. *She grows fat on thwarting her patients: I know it.* Of course, if your strength equalled your disgust, you wouldn't *be* thwarted; you'd obstinately persist in admiring everything she did, though she should comb your hair with a red-hot poker, but being sick and babyish, one can only whimper; and there is where they have us.

"Ill-natured article." Well, suppose it is an ill-natured article? Am I to be the only saint in the world? Am I to pussy-cat round a subject, and never show my claws, or stick up my back, when I catch sight of the enemy! I cry you mercy; in that case I should have been devoured long ago. Beside, wasn't the handle broken off a lovely little porcelain "gift cup" this morning? and isn't it raining cats and dogs, though I *must* go out? and are not these as good reasons for making somebody uncomfortable as *you* had, Sir, or *you*, Madam, for that little thing you did or said this morning to some poor soul in your power, who couldn't resent it? Please get out of your own glass-house before you throw stones at mine.

"But there are good, kind nurses." Well, I am

glad to hear it. Upon my soul, I believe it. Since you say so, and I have had my growl out, I think I remember two or three. They'll go to heaven, of course. What more do you want?

———•••———

A REASONABLE BEING.—If there's anything I hate, it is "a reasonable being." Says the lazy mother to her restless child whom she has imprisoned within doors and whose active mind seeks solutions of passing remarks, "Don't bother, Tommy; do be *reasonable*, and not tease with your questions." Says the husband to his sick or overtasked wife, when she cries from mere mental or physical exhaustion, "How I hate tears; do be a reasonable being." Says the conservative father to his son, whom he would force into some profession or employment for which nature has utterly disqualified him, "Are you wiser than your father? do be a reasonable being." Says the mother to sweet sixteen, whom she would marry to a sixty-five-year old money-bag, "Think what a thing it is to have a fine establishment; do be a reasonable being."

As near as I can get at it, to be a reasonable being, is to laugh when your heart aches; it is to give confidence and receive none; it is faithfully to keep your own promises, and never mind such a trifle as having promises broken to you. It is never to have or to promulgate a dissenting opinion. It is either to be born a fool, or in lack of that to become a hypocrite, trying to become a "reasonable being."

DO AMERICAN WOMEN LOVE NATURE?

I READ an article in *The Nation* the other day, in which the writer deplores "that American women are not lovers of Nature." Now, sins enough both of omission and commission are laid to their charge, without adding to the list those that are baseless. "American women not lovers of Nature!" Where does the writer keep his eyes, that he does not see, even here in the city, in mid-winter, the parlor-windows of almost every house he passes, decorated by the American ladies who preside over it, with hanging baskets of flowering plants, with ivies and geraniums tastefully arranged, besides bouquets of fresh-cut flowers always upon the mantel? Even the humblest house will have its cracked pitcher filled with green moss; as if unwilling to do without that little suggestion of Nature, although the fingers which tend it are coarse with washing, or sewing on shirts at six cents apiece. Did the writer never notice the "American women" going up and down Broadway? How impossible it is for them to resist stopping at the street corners to invest a few pennies in the little fragrant bunch of pansies or tuberoses, for private delectation, and the adornment of their own pretty rooms at home! Then, too, I am a great haunter of green-houses and florists' shops generally; whom, by the way, I consider in the light of missionaries in this work-a-day world, to educate and stimulate our artistic propensities, by the various and beautiful arrangements of form and color, in their floral offerings; and I find there plenty of "American women" enthusiastic in their praises and lavish in their expenditures in this direction. Many of them are flowers themselves, bright, beautiful, lovely, beyond all the buds and sprays and tinted leaves they hover over, like so many humming-birds.

Then, again, when I go into the country each summer, I find "American ladies" rambling in the woods, with a keen appreciation of Nature in all its varied forms, from a lovely sunrise to the last faint chirp of the sleepiest little bird who is safely nestled for the night in his leafy little home. I meet them too in the odorous warm autumn noons, with branches and garlands of gay-tinted leaves, so embarrassed with their wealth of richness that they cannot carry more, and yet unwilling to leave so many "*real beauties*" still trembling, unplucked, on the boughs above them. I see them taking infinite pains to press these bright leaves in books prepared for the purpose, that they may beautify their homes for the cold winter days. Sometimes the result of this painstaking is seen in the form of an ingenious lamp-shade, far more beautiful than one could purchase for any amount of money. Then, again, it will be in the leafy frame for a favorite picture;

then again in a vase, the grouping of branches and tints in such perfect taste, that the most trained artistic eye could find no flaw or blemish.

Now, with all due deference to *The Nation*, in which this article appeared, I beg leave most emphatically to express a difference in opinion; the more so as this increasing interest in floral decorations, particularly those of the parlor windows, has been a matter of great congratulation with me; since the latter gives pleasure to many a passer-by who has neither the means nor time to spend in aught save the bare necessities of life. How many times I have seen some ragged little shivering child stand, spell-bound, before some sunlit window, gay with blossoming plants, and forgetting for the time the dirt and chill and squalor of her own wretched home! How many times the weary seamstress, resting her bundle upon the fence outside, while her eyes drank in their freshness! How many times the laboring man, with his little child beside him, have I seen, as he raised him upon his shoulder to "see the pretty flowers." And *this* is principally why I rejoice that American women *do* love Nature. Those people who stop to look from the outside, are being educated the while to the beautiful, quite unknown to themselves; and these ladies are providing them this pleasure without cost.

I was very much struck, while in Newport last summer, with the educating effect of the superb floral decorations about the villas of the wealthy in that place; for no house there, how humble soever, but had its little emulative patch of bright flowers, or its climbing vines, or its window bouquet. No, no; *The Nation* must have been taking a Rip Van Winkle nap, I think, when it made this unfounded charge against " American Women."

GOOD-NIGHT.—How commonplace is this expression, and yet what volumes it may speak for all future time! We never listen to it, in passing, that this thought does not force itself upon us, be the tones in which it is uttered ever so gay. The lapse of a few fatal hours or minutes may so surround and hedge it in with horror, that of all the millions of words which a lifetime has recorded, these two little words alone shall seem to be remembered.

Good-night!

The little child has lisped it, as it passed, smiling, to a brighter morn than ours; the lover, with his gay dreams of the nuptial morrow; the wife and mother, with all the tangled threads of household care still in her fingers; the father, with the appealing eye of childhood all unanswered.

Good-night!

That seal upon days passed, and days to come. What hand so rash as to rend aside the veil that covers its morrow?

RAINY-DAY PLEASURES.

I LIKE a rainy day. None of your drizzling, half-and-half affairs, but an uncompromising, driving, wholesale, gusty whirlwind of water, that comes rattling, pell-mell, against the windows, that floods sidewalks, and swells gutters, and turns umbrellas inside out, and gives the trees a good shaking. I am sure on that day of slippers and a morning dress till bedtime. I am sure of time to look over the piles of magazines and newspapers that have been accumulating. I can answer some of those haunting letters, or write autographs; I can loll and think; I can put that wretched-looking desk to rights; I can polish up that time-worn gold pen; I can empty and refill my inkstand. I can do a thousand necessary things which a bright, sunshiny day would veto. Of course I don't want it to keep on raining a month. I shall want to wake some day and find a bright sky and clean pavements; but meanwhile I delight in these rattling windows, which make the bright coal-fire look so pleasant, and secure to me an uninterrupted morning; for whoso robs me of my morning, robs me of that which does not enrich him, and leaves me poor indeed. After midday, "come one, come all," etc. But how to make anybody save a writer understand this, is the question. Why you can't write at another portion of the day just as well; why you can't make an exception in their particular case; why an interruption of half an hour or an hour more or less in the morning should matter—this is incomprehensible to persons who, at the same time, would think you quite an idiot, should you undertake to explain to them why uncorked champagne should be after a while flat and stale. "But I can't come at any other time," once urged a person, with more frankness than consideration, who came on her own personal business. Now it is very disagreeable to be obliged to say "no" more than once to the same person; and yet when one's necessary and imperative arrangements of time are disregarded, it is manifestly pardonable. It is a curious fact, however, that authors themselves, who better than anybody else should understand the necessities of the case, are often culpable in this regard; they who, more than anybody else, revel in rainy mornings, or any morning which secures to them uninterrupted time and thought. I am not sure, after all my preaching, of not doing the same thing myself. If I should, I trust nobody will have any scruples about turning me out.

CHIT-CHAT WITH SOME OF MY CORRESPONDENTS.

THE epistles which public persons receive, if published, would not be credible. Begging letters are a matter of course; often in the highwayman style of, "hand over and deliver." I had one recently from a perfect stranger, who wished a cool hundred or so, and mapped out the circuitous way in which it was to be sent, so that "his folks needn't know it," with a belief in my spooniness, which an acquaintance with me would scarcely have warranted. Following close on the heels of this, came another from a woman, whose ideas of my spare time and common-sense were about equally balanced. This stranger of the female persuasion, being hard-up for amusement, wished "a long, racy letter from me, such as I alone could write, with no religion in it, because she got enough of that from the minister's wife." It is unnecessary to add that both these missives found a home in my waste-paper basket. Autograph letters I do not object to, as they keep me in postage stamps, and my little "Bright Eyes" in cards to draw dogs and horses upon.

A friend of mine has been delivered from manuscripts sent for perusal, with the modest accompanying request to find a publisher for the same, by stating her price to be $200. She has received no request of the kind since this announcement.

These are some of the annoyances of authors; but, verily, they have their rewards too. Here comes a letter from my native State, Maine, with a box of wood mosses and berries to place round the roots of my house-plants; and as an expression of affection from a stranger who knows from my writings how well I love such things. She says, in closing, that she hopes that myself and Mr. Beecher will continue to write so long as she lives to read. Mr. Beecher may step up and take his half of this sugarplum, since he has announced himself a champion of "candy."

Then before me on my desk is a smiling baby face sent by its parents, who are strangers to me, if those can be strangers whose hearts warm toward each other; sent me, they add, "not for a silver cup, but because some chance words of mine touched their hearts, and so this little one was named Fanny Fern."

She smiles down upon me whether my sky be cloudy or clear, and in the light of that smile I will try to write worthily; for "their angels do always behold the face of my Father."

Here lie two letters on my desk from strangers regarding an article of mine. One warmly indorses the sentiments therein expressed, and calls upon "God to bless me" for their expression. The other dissents entirely, and commends me to the notice of a *far different Power*, for disseminating such wrong-headed notions. Thank you both! I am used to both styles of epistles. There's nothing I contend for more than individuality of opinion; this would be a stupid world enough if we all thought, felt, and acted after one universal programme; everybody must see things from their own standpoint and through their own spectacles; and, provided they use civil language, should "have the floor" in turn to air their ideas. It might be well to suggest that, in commenting on a newspaper article, care should be taken that it be first thoroughly read, that the writer's meaning be not misinterpreted; if this were done in many cases, the foundation for an adverse opinion would be quite knocked from under. Authors must expect the penalties as well as the rewards of their labors; but one of the most trying is to be accused of sentiments and feelings which they hold in utter abhorrence. Still, he would make small progress on a journey, who should stop to hurl a stone at every barking creature at his heels; therefore, in such cases, let patience have her perfect work, and let the victim keep steadily moving on, with an eye fixed upon the goal in the distance. But when you have unintentionally wounded a gentle spirit, which grieves all the more because it conscientiously believes that you have done harm, ah! then, none would be sorrier than the present writer; none would go farther to soothe the hurt; none would try harder to agree in opinion, consistently with self-respect. But if every writer stopped to consider whether his readers would be pleased, or the contrary, with his sentiments, instead of busying himself with the subject on hand for the moment, it would be like the clouding in of the sun on a clear morning. Everything would be reduced to one colorless level. The bright tints taken away, made brighter by the sometime shadows, could give a landscape tame enough, spiritless enough, to engender hypochondria. Surely the world of to-day is more liberal than this. Surely it is learning "to agree to differ." Surely it knows by this time that a good life is of more importance than creeds or beliefs. Surely in this year of our Lord, 1867, the days of the Inquisition are past both for editors and writers, and the watchword of to-day—and, thank God, for to-morrow, and the day after—is progress, not paralysis.

Having said this, I consider that I have cleared the deck for action, as far as my own ship is concerned. A stray shot won't frighten or discourage me; on the contrary, it only makes me step round the livelier, to see that my guns are in working order. Then, again, any one who wishes to hail me, and haul alongside in a friendly manner, shall be always certain of a kind salute from me.

A lady whose life, like that of many others, has not run smoothly through a bed of flowers, writes me "to tell her the secret of courage, which she is sure I know."

I do not profess to speak for others, but the secret of all the courage I ever had is a firm belief in immortality, and in its satisfactory unriddling of this life of *seeming* cross-purposes. Without this I can never tell how either man or woman can learn to look their dead in the face, or what is oftener much harder to do, to look their living in the face. I can never tell how they can lay their distracted heads upon their pillows at night, without praying that they may never wake to another sunrise, or how they can stagger to their feet seventy times seven, after prostrations of body and spirit, which come one after another, like the blows of some avenging fiend. I cannot tell else how they can see the good crushed and defeated and apparently extinguished, and the unscrupulous and bad receiving all homage, and sitting triumphant in high places. I cannot tell else how the wretched mother can take, lovingly and patiently, to her heart *another* little one, when her failing strength is already tasked to the utmost to care for little brothers and sisters, who, having a father, are yet fatherless. It must be only because *her* eyes can see clearly "Our Father who art in heaven." I look with sorrowing wonder upon those who, passing in and out of their pleasant, and as yet unbroken, homes, refuse to see the marks of blood upon their door-post, betokening the death of the first-born. I marvel that these steppers upon flowers childishly make no provision for the pitfalls concealed beneath them. I wonder at those who, laying their treasure all up in *one* place, never think, in this world of change, of the day of bankruptcy.

I do *not* wonder, when their household gods are shivered, that such exclaim, " Ye have taken away my idols, and *what have I left?* " or that suicide or lunacy are often the results.

It is only they who, in such crises, believe in " Him who doeth all things well," that have anything " left." It is only such who have courage for what sorrow soever is yet in store for them, in a life which for the moment seems robbed of all its sunshine. It is only they who have learned to live out of themselves, and who can yield—tearfully it may be, but unrepiningly—their earthly hopes and treasures up.

This is all the " courage " I know which will help us to look upon the dear dead face with patient resignation, or take up again the next morning the weary, vexed burden of life, until we are summoned to lay it down.

Lucia:—I am sorry that in your innocence you should have placed any dependence upon the statements of " a New York Correspondent." It is a pity to pull down any of the fine air-castles they are in the habit of building; still it is my duty to inform you that these gentry often describe, with the greatest minuteness, authors and authoresses whom they have never seen, manufacturing at the same time little personal histories concerning these celebrities, valuable only as ingenious specimen-" bricks, made without straw." It matters little to the writers whether nature has furnished the authoress about whom they romance with black eyes or blue, brown hair or flaxen; whether nature made her a six-foot grenadier, or a symmetrical pocket edition of womanhood; the description answers all the same for the provincial paper for which it was intended, and these Ananias and Sapphira gentry find that a spicy lie pays as well as the truth—at least till they are found out. No, madam; notwithstanding the statements of your valuable "New York Correspondent" for the ———, I have no "daughters married;" I never "wear a black stocking on one foot and a white one on the other, at the same time, to attract attention;" I never "rode on the top of an omnibus;" I don't "smoke cigarettes or chew opium;" I have no personal knowledge concerning the "mud-scow," "handcart," "cooking stove," and "hotel," that you have his authority for saying have been severally "named for me." I am not "married to Mr. Bonner," who has a most estimable wife of his own. I "never delivered an address in public;" and with regard to "the amount I have made by my pen," you and the special "New York Correspondent" are quite at liberty to speculate about it, without any assistance from me. As to my "religious creed," the first article in it is, "Thou shalt not bear false witness against thy neighbor."

A gentleman writes me to know "if it is true that I boldly, and unwinkingly, and unblushingly stated, over my own signature, and contrary to the usual custom of my sex, that I was fifty-eight years old."

Well, sir, I did. Why not? I feel prouder of that fact, and of my being the grandmother of the handsomest and smartest grandchild in this or any other country, than of any other two facts I have knowledge of. I can't conceive why men, or women either—for this squeamishness about one's age, I find, is not at all a thing of sex—should care one penny about it. I say again, I *am* "fifty-eight," and I am glad of it. I have had my day, and I am quite willing that every other woman should have hers.

WILL PARENTS TAKE HEED?—On all hands complaints are made of the increasing ill-health of our school-children. Now who is to take this matter in hand? Who is to say there shall be absolutely *no* lessons learned out of school, unless the present duration of school hours shall be shortened? It needs, we think, only that the parents shall themselves *insist* upon this to effect it. Why wait till brain-fever has set in? Why wait till little spines are irretrievably crooked? And of what mortal use is it to keep on pouring anything into a vessel when it is incapable of holding any more, and is only wasted upon the ground?

MY LIKING FOR PRETTY THINGS.

"H, you luxurious puss!" That remark was addressed to me, because I said I would like to be lulled to sleep each night, and awoke each morning by strains of sweet music. There's no harm in imagining things, I hope, provided one goes quietly and ploddingly on in what the ministers call "the path of duty." Now, for instance, sometimes I amuse myself planning beautiful forms for dishes, and cups, and plates, and glasses; beautiful patterns for carpets and wall-papers; beautiful and odd frames for pictures; beautiful loopings and draperies for window-curtains; and beautiful shapes for chairs and tables. Sometimes I eat an imaginary breakfast in a room with long windows, opening out into a lovely garden full of sweet flowers; like lilies of the valley and roses and mignonette and heliotrope and violets—oh, yes! violets *everywhere*. Then those lovely "pond lilies" should grow in the water, at the bottom of the garden, and some of them should be brought in, fresh, dewy, and cool, and placed on the breakfast-table; and little birds should hop in, over the threshold of the breakfast-room, for crumbs, and sing me a song of thanks; and a great, monstrous dog should lie prone upon the piazza; and vines should wreathe themselves round the pillars thereof; clematis and sweet pea, and honeysuckles, white and red, and the gorgeous trumpet-flower; and nobody should be able to find the chimneys at all, for the lovely blooming Wisteria that should clamber over the roof. *Such* trees and such velvet grass as I'd have around the house! Giant horse-chestnuts and elms and oaks and maples; and here and there a lovely statue peeping out in some unexpected place. And then I'd invite you, and you, and you; not because I would like to make a show-thing of it, but because I would like to see you enjoy it as much as myself.

Wouldn't it be nice? I *do* hate *ugly* things—there's no use in denying it. Sometimes Mr. Librario brings in one of his profound books, and lays it, *pro tem.*, on my parlor-table; he looks for it shortly, and finds it not. "I knew it would be banished when I put it there," he says, "because the binding was so homely."

He pretends, too, that water tastes just as cool poured out from an ugly-shaped pitcher as out of my pet china one, with the graceful lip, and vine-wreathed sides and handle; and when I send for "a headache-cup-of-tea," and add, "Now be sure you bring it in my lovely blue-tinted cup-and-saucer," he laughs, and asks, "if *that* will make my head any better?" Why, of course it will. Now, you see, if I, like a coward, dodged work and bother, and the disagreeables of life, when they had to be met, that would be one thing; but I don't; I just take 'em vigorously by the horns till I get through with them; and so I maintain that I have a right to my luxurious dreams and my *pretties*, if they do me any good. Now haven't I? And speaking of that, as I was looking round the other day, I saw such a dreadful waste of ingenuity that my heart bled for the misapplied talent of the inventor. It was a straw-colored butter-dish in the shape of a *man's hat*, ribbon and all complete. The rim thereof did duty as a saucer, while the divorcible crown was clapped over the butter. Horrible! Then I saw an egg dish, with an executive *sitting* hen, awfully natural, doing duty as a cover. I left the locality abruptly, fearing I might see a meat-dish cover, in the form of a pig—snout, tail, bristles and all.

Why, I ask in this connection, am I daily tortured with the sight of lamps supported by bronze cherubs, appealing piteously to my wide-awake maternal instincts? And why are my evenings at public places of amusement spoiled by the sight of galleries of heartless people held up whole evenings by wretchedly carved female figures, in every stage of contorted legs, knees, heads, and arms.

"Didn't I tell you that it would be better if you hadn't quite so much imagination," triumphantly retorts Mr. Cynic.

Very true, you did; but still I don't agree with you; because looking at *some* people through that glorified medium, I have been able to discover virtues—which—otherwise——Yes, sir!

UNSOUGHT HAPPINESS.

OLD stagers know that the way to be happy is to give up all attempts to be so. In other words, the cream of enjoyment in this life is always impromptu. The *chance* walk; the unexpected visit; the unpremeditated journey; the unsought conversation or acquaintance.

Everybody feels more or less conscious in their "Sunday clothes." Who does not know the blessing of comfortable everyday apparel, every fold of which has made intimate acquaintance with the motions and postures of the owner; and which can be worn without fear of being spoiled, or rendering the wearer conspicuous. The bonnet which sets lightly on the head and defies rain; the boots which do not constantly remind the foot that a chair would be the greatest of all earthly blessings; in short, that freedom which will let you forget *you* yourself, is like laying down a huge bundle which has fettered you weary miles on a dusty, sunny road, and sitting down, unencumbered, in a shady spot to dream and rest in a delicious, care-free coolness. It is just so with the mind. The best things written or spoken have *not* been written or spoken "to order." They "*whistled themselves,*" as the terror-stricken urchin remarked to his irate schoolma'am. They came unbidden, in easy, flowing raiment; not starched and stately, rustling, prim, and conscious. They came without thought of "what people would say." They stepped out because the time had come when they *couldn't stay in*. In a word, they were *natural* as little children are, and consequently delicious and fresh.

I solemnly aver that, the moment anybody *tries* to do or say a good thing, that moment he shall never be delivered of it, but shall only experience throes of mortal pain trying. If you build yourself a beautiful house, and make it a marvel of taste and convenience, in one of its lovely chambers shall your dead be laid; and you shall wander heart-sick away from it, to rid yourself of a phantom that will always follow you, till you turn boldly and face it, and with a strong heart accept its company.

This incessant *striving* to be happy! Never, never shall mortals be so till they have learned to give it over. Happiness *comes*. It will not be challenged. It glides in only when you have closed the door and turned your back upon it, and forgot it. It lays a soft hand on your face when you thought to be alone, and brings a joyful flush of surprise to your cheek, and a soft light to your weary eye, and ineffable peace to your soul.

It is a great thing when all that can possibly happen to a person, save one's death, *has* happened. It is a great thing to have been poor, and friendless, and nameless, and to have been rich, and famous, and flattered. It is a great thing to have been young and to have been old. It is a great thing to have perforated the bubble, Fame, and seen it collapse before a hungry heart. It is a great thing to have had dear ones, who moulded every thought and action, from the rising to the setting sun, and then to have seen them suddenly vanish like stars from the sky, and to have folded one's paralyzed hands in the darkness because there was no earthly future left. It is a great thing to have suffered and agonized in your own Gethsemane on account of it, till that very suffering brings you to be glad and contented that *they* are in a world where all tears are wiped from all eyes. It is a great thing to rise slowly and take up the burden of life again and plod mechanically on. It is a great thing to be calm and unmoved when brutal pens, to point a coarse paragraph, unearth one's sacred dead. It is a great thing to lock up chambers in one's soul, and sit down by the closed doors, lest some apathetic or unkind ear should hear the pained cries you only want time to smother. It is a great thing to have encountered all of malice, and envy, and uncharitableness, that the world has to offer, so that its repetition can only be to the ear a dull, unmeaning sound. It is a great thing so to have weighed human judgment that its Aye or No is a matter of indifference in the light of—*to come.*

True; before the sensitive and tender-hearted can reach that point, rivers of tears must have been shed and millions of sighs heaved. Scores of suns must have set on days of torturing length, and scores of mornings *too many* must have dawned. Uncounted hours must have been spent reaching out in the darkness for that which the soul has never found, or, finding, has lost; and thousands of times must the weary hands have fallen to the side in utter helplessness.

But this churchyard of the soul passed through, where every step is upon some buried hope, what is the petty noise and dust of the highway about which others fume and complain? What is it to the unconscious if rudely jostled in passing? What is it if a malicious whipster spatter mud? What is it if a rude voice accost, or the right of the road be clamorously contended? when all voices, all roads are alike; when delay or speed matters not; when a choice about *anything* seems utterly ridiculous, and all one's faculties are lost in astonishment at the worry and fret and perturbation of those who have not undergone the same ossifying process as yourself.

After all, some great sorrow is surely essential to the humanizing of every soul. Never till then can it offer anything but lip sympathy to those who have gasped through the sea of trouble. How can he who has known only days of comparative prosperity interpret the despairing sigh of the friendless? How can he who has never dropped tears into the open grave of *his own dead* measure the agony of that last, lingering look, as they are hidden forever from human sight? Till a vacant chair stands by his own hearth, how can he ever understand why one should still keep on grieving for that which can never be recalled? Till his heart turns sickening away from some festive anniversary in which a missing voice once made music, how can he see why one need be doleful on such a day as that? Till he has closed his ears to some familiar strain which evoked associations too painful to bear, how can he tell "Why you cannot forget all that, since it makes you so miserable"? To answer such, is to talk to the blind of colors, to the deaf of sounds, to the dead of life and motion. Never, till his own house is darkened, till the badge of desolation flutters from his own door, till sunshiny days return merciless in their brightness, and stormy ones send his thoughts shuddering to a shelterless grave; never till he has tried changing the place, but still *always* only to keep the old pain, can he understand the desperation with which at last one sits helplessly down, to face that which it can neither look upon nor flee from.

DIGNITY OF HUMAN NATURE.

THE philosopher is fond of talking to me about what he calls "the dignity of human nature." The pains he takes to bolster himself up in this shaky belief of his, would do credit to a better cause. Obstinacy of course is at the bottom of it, for he no more believes in it than I do. How can he, and he living and breathing in this sublunary sphere *himself?* That's just what I said to him this morning; for, thank Providence, I can generally speak my mind on most points. What did he say? That's my affair; suffice it to say, he sticks to it. I made him sit down; then I sat down on his knee, to make sure of a listener. Then I took in my hand the morning papers. In the first place, there was a man of sixty who had been coaxed in where he shouldn't go, and robbed while there. Secondly, there was a justice of the peace sentenced to the Penitentiary for robbery. Thirdly, there was a clergyman convicted of bigamy. Fourthly, there was a husband, who had been trying, with an iron shovel, to find out whether his wife had any brains. Fifthly, there was another who had decided an argument by biting off a portion of his antagonist's nose. Sixthly, there were two lads, of the respective ages of eight and thirteen, who had been murderously perforating each other's intestines with sharp penknives. Seventhly, there was a man in Massachusetts who had lately numbered his twenty-fifth child. Eighthly, there was a "gentleman" found, in the small-hours, sitting on the cold sidewalk in —— street, hiccupping for a waiter " to bring him another bottle of champagne."

"Well," says the philosopher, when I stopped to take breath, "these are only the exceptions that prove the rule." Exceptions, quotha! when I hadn't yet dug into the nauseous kennel of the advertising list! *Exceptions?* but what's the use of talking? Does not every morning's new issue furnish similar "exceptions"? Certainly. Besides, didn't I put *this* catechism to him? How came —— to give the wife of an official high in power that splendid grand piano? There's a *dignified* way to secure, through a wheedling female tongue, a fat office. Not to mention a carriage and horses unexpectedly placed at the disposal of Senator ——'s wife. Last, but not least, look at "Jeff.," first and last, from his attempted flight to his boyish refusal to eat his prison fare, bestowing it gratuitously in the faces of his guards; and then kicking and swearing, while his naughty little hands and feet were being fastened together therefor. Dignity? when I look at human beings, and think of what they daily and hourly do, I am seized with convulsions of laughter at the idea. Sometimes the devil possesses me, in the presence of some solemn "hark from the tombs" kind of an individual, to picture it, till I am tied up with cramps trying to keep from laughing. Nobody will ever know what I've suffered in this way. Dignity? You should see it with its boots up on the window-sill of some hotel lounging-room facing Broadway, with its mouth wide open, thus—O; its hat rakishly set on one temple, and its eyes somnolently closed to the charms of the lady pedestrians, who wouldn't miss the picture for sixpence. Dignity? Yesterday I saw a man nearly cut in two with corsets. Another trying to hop round hilariously in a pair of corn-murdering boots. Another roaring out in an omnibus like a mad bull because the cold-fingered driver gave him a "soiled stamp."

Dignity of human nature? Where is it when a man is in the dentist's chair? Where, when a waiter spills coffee on his shirt-bosom or hot soup on his trousers? One might as well not stiffen himself up against facts like these, said I to the philosopher. We don't stop being children, this side the grave, that ever I could find out. The toys we mostly scramble for, like those that dangle from the Christmas-tree, suit but the present hour, and, with all their gilding and glittering lights, will one day be but broken rubbish on our hands. When a man is dead he looks dignified; but while he is alive, with a pipe stereotyped to his lips, or alternately dipping his *soup*-erfluous mustache in a plate of soup and sopping it with a napkin; or, as the countrywoman said of her pet minister, "sitting down, spitting round socionable," I really can't entertain the idea of "Dignity." The more I try the more I laugh. Frivolous, I grant; but what were woman without frivolity? Not a man would speak to us.

———•◆•———

WHAT MINISTERS NEED.—We have often thought that ministers need their congregations as much, if not more, than congregations need their ministers. Parishioners are not apt to look at it in this way. The matter of salary nowadays, thank God, is, as a general thing, properly considered; but the matter of "holding up his hands" spiritually, is not. Remember, he is a man like yourselves, subject to discouragement, and needs—oh, more often than you know who only look on his face once a week—that affectionate relationship which you delight in between your own children and yourself. You wish their respect, but would you be satisfied with only that? Do you not delight in the beaming eye and constant, kindly, heartfelt recognition of your presence? Just so your minister feels toward you, else he were no minister. Then do not treat him as you would a Fourth-of-July orator, or a stray lecturer, to be paid and dismissed, and forgotten when his message is delivered, careless after that whether he be crushed or shipwrecked on his way home. Remember the phrase, "holding up his hands." It has a world of significance, looked at in this light.

ALL ABOUT DOCTORS.

THERE be many kinds of Doctors; allopathic—homœpathic—and mongrel. Luckily every family swears by its own, and believes in no salvation beyond *his* dictum. There is your fashionable Doctor who lives in a fine house; rides to his "cases" with a servant in livery; utterly eschews all gutter localities, and never troubles himself to go out when his head aches, or in bad weather. His manner of drawing off his gloves is pompous and impressive. Nurse in the corner sinks down into her slippers, utterly quenched by it. While he warms his hands silently at the fire, he is impressing all present with an idea of his immense profundity. This done, he fixes his eyes on the ceiling, and counts his patient's pulse; then comes the tongue examination; after which he relapses into another profound contemplation of the ceiling; during which time every tick of the clock seems solemn as fate. Then follows the cabalistic writing; a dead letter to everybody but this Grand Mogul and the apothecary. The gloves are then drawn on, and bowing to the thin air, our elegant Doctor delivers himself again into the care of his liveried servant.

Then there is your old-fashioned Doctor; whose patients "will have him," though he has wanted gradually to leave off practice for several years, in favor of new aspirants. The cut of his coat is a matter that don't affect his practice. He smiles blandly as the other Doctor, with the liveried servant, drives past, while he trudges independently on foot, and mentally shakes his head at "new fashions." *He* is civil without regard to externals. A baby is a baby to him, whether it comes into the world with a nice wardrobe ready for its back, or the contrary. He is perfectly willing to tell a man who places his stomach in his hands what he is going to put into it, and what he expects it to do to him. He is interested philanthropically, as well as scientifically, in the most minute symptom of the most ordinary patient, who is encouraged by the sympathetic magnetism of his voice and eye to "tell him just how he feels." He scribbles no unnecessary recipes for his own benefit, or the apothecaries'; and speaks so cheerfully when he leaves, that the sick man half doubts, after all, if anything is the matter with him.

Then there is your young, new-fledged Doctor, who gives physic as a little boy touches off a firecracker, rather uncertain whether it will blow him, or his neighbor, or both, sky-high.

Then there is your Ladies' Doctor, "the handsome creature," who lifts his eyes with well-acted astonishment that these dear beings can endure a pain, or an ache, and still live; who says just what they want him to, in the way of prescribing "little journeys" and savory messes; and coaxes all their little troubles over their lips till they are more astonished at themselves than the Doctor is at them.

Then there is your blunt pop-gun Doctor, who has no time nor inclination for nonsense, and jerks out his opinion as he would a mouthful of tobacco; and they who don't like it, are welcome to move out of the way. Who feels your pulse, and pronounces you a prospective dead man, or woman, as coolly as if the intelligence concerned you no more than himself.

Then there is the eccentric Doctor, who advertises himself by some peculiarity of costume, like knee-breeches, or cocked hat, or long, flowing hair, and is never better pleased than when everybody is saying: "Who *can* that be?"

Then there is your celebrated Surgeon, who has long since bade good-by to his own nerves, and who looks at every man, woman, and child with a view to their "cutting up." When about to commence an operation before a class of gaping students, mark the gleaming, circling flourish of his pet-knife in the air, before descending upon his chloroform-bound victim! The operation properly and deftly performed, *his* part is done. The Almighty is responsible for the rest.

Finally, and lastly, it is all very nice to laugh at Doctors when one is sound and well; but let a good smart pain come, and none so ready, as those who do so, to send a telegraphic summons for their speedy appearance. With this substantial proof of their power, let them snap their fingers at criticism and be jolly.

How to Put the Children to Bed.—*Not* with a reproof for any of that day's sins of omission or commission. Take any other time *but* bedtime for that. If you ever heard a little creature sighing or sobbing in its sleep, you could never do this. Seal their closing eyelids with a kiss and a blessing. The time will come, all too soon, when they will lay their heads upon their pillows lacking both. Let them then at least have this sweet memory of a happy childhood, of which no future sorrow or trouble can rob them. Give them their rosy *youth*. Nor need this involve wild license. The judicious parent will not so mistake my meaning. If you have ever met the man or the woman whose eyes have suddenly filled when a little child has crept trustingly to its mother's breast, you may have seen one in whose childhood's home "Dignity" and "Severity" stood where Love and Pity should have been. Too much indulgence has ruined thousands of children; too much *Love* not one.

LETTER TO HENRY WARD BEECHER.

"There has been a very jolly set of children in my house since the box [of mixed candies] came. I have made a scientific analysis with such means as I had at hand—my tongue and palate —and am of opinion that it is pure, and am sure that it is *good* (I know that Fanny Fern is sorry that she ever wrote a word against candy, and stands pouting, to think that I have all the sweets on my side)."—*Mr. Beecher in N. Y. Ledger.*

POUTING? Not a bit of it. After I make up my mind a thing is past being helped, I always turn my giant mind to something else.

Now, "your riverence," your love for "sweets" is not a thing of yesterday. I mind me of a young man, of your name, who once came to a boarding-school, where I, at sixteen, was placed for algebra and safe-keeping, both of which I hated, and who invited me to take several surreptitious rides with him, which I did; and which will probably first come to the knowledge of his sister, my teacher, through this number of the New York *Ledger*. What Plymouth church has escaped, in the way of an infliction, by that young man's going to college about that time, and my return to the "bosom of my family," to learn the "Lost Arts," bread-making and button-hole stitching, Plymouth church may now for the first time learn.

And now, having paid you off for your little public dig at me, I proceed magnanimously to admit, that I believe a bit of *pure* candy, given to a child as dessert after a wholesome meal, is perfectly harmless. But not even the gifted pastor of Plymouth church, whose sermons, to me, are like a spring of water in the desert, can ever make me believe that an indiscriminate nibble of even *pure* candy between meals is good for any child.

Now, Mr. Beecher, we are both grandfathers—I mean, *you* are a grandfather, and I am a grandmother. I now propose to pit my grandchild against yours on the candy question, and see which, in the future, brings us the heaviest dentist and doctor's bills. We won't scratch each other's eyes out now, both on account of "auld lang syne," and on account of the dignity of our position—I mean the dignity of *yours*.

I have one thing against you besides candy, and that is, that I can never get a seat at your church. As everybody is giving you advice, of which, by the way, I too have plenty, I advise you to remove to New York, that I may be able, without getting up in the middle of the night in order to cross the ferry, to get a seat in one of your pews. You have been in Brooklyn now for a long time, and if the people over there haven't yet become angels, it is high time you tried your hand on the other kind in New York.

I propose the site of the present Bible House, as being a nice walk from my residence, which is the main thing to be considered. I will agree to find your pulpit in flowers—(not of oratory; that is for you!)

Hoping that you will be able to turn from your beloved box of candy to an early consideration of this question, I am—leaving out candy—

Your faithful adherent,   FANNY FERN.

ONE KIND OF FOOL.—It is very instructive sometimes, at a place of country resort, to watch the woman who has come only to exhibit her changes of wardrobe. For a day or two, possibly longer, she goes through her solitary dress-rehearsals. Finding at last that the rest of the boarders wear rubbers and water-proofs, and live out of doors in all weathers, the woman who came to dress, gets weary of waiting for admirers, and reluctantly joins the sensible majority, rather than be left alone; but generally with an apologetic, "How odd it seems, not to dress for dinner as one does in the city," by way of letting herself gently down from her snobbish pedestal. We are happy to add, however, that the number of women who go into the country to dress is becoming fewer every year; folly in this regard having reached its ultimatum of loathsomeness.

THE AMENITIES OF THE TABLE.

FASTIDIOUSNESS, in any regard, is a misfortune, as two-thirds of mankind have no such word in their dictionary. But in matters of the table we claim for every human being a large margin of license as to peculiarities of taste. Now *helping at table* is a science. To tact and skill your helper must needs add benevolence. He or she must be capable of comprehending that too large a slice, or too brimming a spoonful, may save the trouble of helping twice, in more ways than one, as it may effectually destroy the appetite. Your helper must not suppose that safely to land a piece of meat on the plate, instead of the table-cloth, his or her duty is done; on the contrary, the boundary line between squash and spinach, cranberry sauce and cauliflower, may be distinctly defined with advantage to many stomachs and palates. Nor must your helper close his or her eyes to the fact that some specified joint, or bone, or slice, may be disagreeable, through some unexplainable though very decided antipathy. Nor must he or she disdain to be informed, if ignorant of the fact, that a bit of butter has a better relish if it be not flattened down on your plate, after the manner of an apothecary spreading a plaster. Then gravy is undoubtedly a meritorious liquid when one has a confidential physician, and money enough to fee him; but as this is not always the case, one may be pardoned for not wishing to have it taken for granted that it is to be soused over his food, without permission. *Once I saw a philanthropic carver.* His patience and assiduity were beyond all praise; but in an evil day, in a philosophical mood, inspecting him too closely with admiring eyes, I discovered the fatal spring of his amiability. It was only a blind for the secretion of his favorite titbits till, his labors over, the delicious process of mastication should commence for *him!* That's what comes of looking too closely into things. It has happened to me before.

The Smiths believe that edibles were made to eat; and that digestion is a humbug invented by the doctors; and that milk and cider, and pastry and vinegar, and candy and raisins, and flapjacks and pickles, and jellies, can be eaten in successive strata at any hour in the twenty-four, and in any condition of body or mind, and repose quietly together like "the Happy Family." The Smiths believe in getting up in the middle of the night to eat and then going to bed upon it; they believe in taking a bath alike on a full or an empty stomach, and they utterly despise exercise. If they are sick, it is never on account of any of *these* barbaric heresies.

Now, the Joneses, having studied physiology, look upon food as a necessary evil. No Rabbi could more utterly sniff down pork. Grease in every form is tabooed; preserves and pastry sent to Coventry, or only set before company, who have an undoubted right to kill themselves if fashion requires it. The Joneses, when helping you at table, always prefix the offered morsel with, Pray take it, it is so healthful; or, It will assist your digestion; or, It is an excellent corrective; till the association between potatoes and physic, meat and medicine, is so intimate, that one ceases to regard these edibles in the light of food. You are cautioned against veal because of necessity it must be *young* meat; against fish, lest it may aggravate a possible scrofulous tendency; against tea, because the leaves may have been dried on copper; against milk, because you are unacquainted with the pedigree of the cow from whence it came. Bread is microscopically inspected for imaginary adulterations, and after all these precautions the timid Joneses, restricted to the simplest forms of two or three permissible and monotonous eatables, swallow even these nervously, and with an eye to the undertaker; and if attacked by headache, submit to it meekly, as a penance for some unknown infringement of nature's law.

Now the Adamses believe in *quantity*, not *quality*. An ounce of paving-stones is as good as an ounce of mutton; in other words, you may eat your grandmother with impunity, if you only confine yourself to a small piece, and are jolly over it. Luckily for butchers, confectioners, grocers, doctors, and sextons, each of these hobbies finds its followers.

8

I believe in eating. The person who affects to despise it either comforts himself with private bites, or is unfitted by disease to eat at all. It does not disenchant me, as it does some, to see "a woman eat." I know that the dear creatures cannot keep up their plumpness on saw-dust, or the last "Lady's Book." I look at them as the future mothers of healthy little children; and I say mentally, Eat, my dears, and be satisfied; but be sure that you take a good walk after you have digested your food. Still there may be limits to one's tolerance even in this regard. The other morning, at a hotel breakfast, I had been contemplating with great interest a fair creature, who took her seat opposite to me, in all the freshness of a maiden's morning toilette. Smooth hair, tranquil brow, blue eyes, and a little neat white collar finishing off a very pretty morning-robe; and here you will permit me to remark that, if women did but know it, but they don't, and never will, a ball-room toilette is nothing to a neat breakfast dress. Well, my fairy read the bill of fare, while I admired the long eyelashes that swept her cheek. Straightway she raised her pretty head, and lisped this order to the colored waiter at her elbow:

"John! Coffee, Fried Pigs' Feet, Fried Oysters, Omelette, Pork Steak."

MANY MEN OF MANY MINDS.

IT is very curious with what different eyes different people may look upon the same object. Not long since a lady and gentleman in travelling arrived at the hotel of one of our largest watering-places just at the dinner-hour. The lady, preferring a warm meal to an elaborate toilette, proposed going in "just as they were." Seating themselves in the places designated by that important personage, the head waiter, they inspected the tempting bill of fare, gave their orders, and bided their time, longer or shorter, for their completion; the hotel being overcrowded, it proved to be *longer*. The lady solaced herself by reviewing the guests. Presently, touching her companion's arm, she exclaimed: "Look! did you ever see a more beautiful woman? Look at her throat, and the poise of her head, and her lovely profile. See! how she smiles! hasn't she a lovely mouth?" "Pshaw!" replied the gentleman, "I dare say she's well enough, but do you suppose that boiled mutton I ordered will ever arrive?"

The other day a beautiful child came into an omnibus with its nurse. It commenced smiling at all the passengers, pointing its tiny forefinger at this one and that, by way of making acquaintance. One old gentleman in the far corner responded by a series of signals with a red-silk pocket handkerchief, to which the social little baby made ready response. Another gentleman near, upon whose newspaper the smiling child laid its hand with trusting fearlessness, looked over his spectacles at it with a frown, gave an ugly grunt, and shortly turned his back, to prevent a repetition of the familiarity.

"How did you like the Rev. Mr. ——'s sermon?" asked a gentleman of another, as they were leaving the church. "Solid gold, every word of it," replied he; "sound doctrine eloquently presented." "Strange!" replied the querist; "for my own part, I was so disgusted, that I could with difficulty keep my seat." "What! a minister raise a smile on the faces of his audience in such a solemn place! I wonder what my old pastor, Dr. Dry-Starch would have thought of such a proceeding! *He* always taught us that this was a solemn world; and that the man who laughed in it might very likely be laughing over the very spot where in time he might be buried."

"How do you like Mr. Theophilus Tennant's new novel?" asked one lady of another. "Well, if you want my honest opinion," replied the latter, "I consider it a shallow, egotistical, inflated affair, whatever paid critics may assert to the contrary." "Possible?" exclaimed the querist; "why, I was so delighted with it that I had serious thoughts of addressing a letter of thanks to the owner for the pleasure he had afforded me, although I never saw or spoke to him."

"What a splendid specimen of a man!" exclaimed Miss Twenty to Mrs. Thirty-five. "It makes one feel stronger and better to be in the same room with him." "Heavens!" exclaimed the matron; "I can think of nothing when I see him but a great, lumbering, overgrown, Newfoundland dog. A man with so much surplus body to look after can't have much time for anything else."

And so we might multiply instances *ad infinitum* (which is about all the Latin I know). For my own part I don't quarrel with that diversity of taste which finds pretty wives for ugly husbands, fine, smart husbands for silly women, full congregations for prosy ministers, overflowing audiences for flat lecturers, and a reading parish, notwithstanding her faults, for Fanny Fern.

MY NOTION OF A WALKING COMPANION.

OF all small miseries, an uncongenial *walking companion* is the most annoying. Some people take a walk as they would study the multiplication table. It is a necessary performance, to be got over as soon as possible. I am not alluding to that class of human oyster, but to those who, after close application, or the exhausting wear and fret of everyday life, feel as though the four walls about them were gradually contracting, and their chance for breath growing fainter and fainter; to whom fresh air and the blue sky are as necessary as is dew and sunshine to flowers; and like them, without which, they as certainly droop and die;—such will understand what I mean by that misused term —*a walk*. Not a dawdle, not a feminine " calling " tour; nor an errand of any sort, for any purpose under heaven, that can be construed into business; but a dreamy lounge, irrespective of anything but the cool feel of the air on the heated temples, and the great, ceaseless, murmuring wave of life beating against the shore of time, bearing you and others on its bosom wheresoever God willeth. People pass you like moving shadows, you hear the pleasant hum of their voices, but do not know in your som-

My Notion of a Walking Companion. 119

nambulistic mood whether they are familiar faces or not. You only thank God for unfettered limbs, and fresh air, and motion; beyond that, for the time being, you desire to know nothing. Ah, *then* —to be unexpectedly linked to some human fidget! Whose limbs jerk this way and that, as if they were pulled by invisible wires; who goes first fast, then slow; then pulls you up with a short jerk to look at something; who bothers you with infinitesimal small talk; who ceaselessly interlards inquiries which chain you remorselessly to the tug-boat of his or her ideas, without leave of mental absence for one reprieving moment; and all this very likely accompanied with the most friendly and amiable intentions on the part of your entertainer (?). To say "No" and "Yes" recklessly—and laugh in the wrong place, and go home a million times more weary than when you started, beside feeling that you have hopelessly excluded yourself from the list of sane human beings—that's what I call misery.

But, ah! the ecstatic bliss of walking with one who thinks with you, as he moves dreamily on without speech—to be free to utter or to be silent, and no offence given or taken. To be allowed to wander leagues off, without fear of being rudely jerked back to time, at any unpropitious moment.

To turn this corner and that, by some mutual magnetic understanding, that you smile at afterward, when you come to think of it, as strangely funny and agreeable. To reach your own door-step as rested and refreshed, and with as cool and tranquil a brow, as if your own mother had sung you to sleep with the old-time nursery lullaby. To go back with fresh heart and spirit, to take up your burden of duty where weary nature had lain it hopelessly down. That's *my* kind of " walk."

There are certain persons whom to meet is like opening the window of a close apartment on a delicious June day. The first breath is an inspiration. You throw back your locks from your heated forehead, and your weary eyes, and ask nothing but to sit down and let this soother minister to you. All your cares, and frets, one by one creep away, and a new life and vigor seem infused into every nerve and muscle. You are not the same creature that you were ten minutes before. You are ready after all to do valiant battle with life, though you had supposed yourself quite surrendered to its everyday, petty, and harassing tyrant necessities. Exuberant animal strength must needs carry with it hopefulness and courage; and they whose nerves have been strained and weakened by past trouble, welcome the breezy, fresh influence of such, like Heaven's own dew and sunshine. It is a tonic, the blessing of which the unconscious giver knows not how to appreciate perhaps, but oh how invaluable to the receiver! A soulful face, an exultant word —a light, springing step! We raise our weary eyes first in wonder, then in admiration; and the sympathetic chord thus struck—the brow clears, the eyes brighten, and life seems—not the curse we morbidly thought it—but the blessing God intended it.

MEN TEACHERS IN GIRLS' SCHOOLS.

I AM inclined to think, with all due deference to the powers that be, that *male* teachers are not best for young girls. It takes a woman, who understands all the witcheries of the sex, and off whom they glance harmless, like water off a turtle's back, to deal with these young kittens; they have more fun than geography can absorb, and are not to be feruled like a great cub of a boy, whose whole future life will be license after jacketdom, as decreed by society and the laws; while a severe woman-discipline surely awaits the most frolicsome girl, beginning from the moment when she first learns what her heart is made of, till death stills its yearnings.

And yet I pity a male teacher of girls, whose studied dignity is in a second dethroned by a single pantomimic gesture of some bright-eyed young flirt, who *feels* her power without yet being old enough to understand it, and with an instinctive coquetry gets on his blind side, turning all his fore-ordained frowns into ill-suppressed smiles. How can he box those little round ears? How can he disfigure those soft, white palms? How can he—sending all the other pupils home—trust himself, after school, alone with those bright eyes, to put them through a subduing tear process? Ten to one the "subduing" is on the other side!

Said I to a little girl, not many mornings since, who was getting ready for school, "Why do you put on that bright new dress to go, when your old brown one would do as well?" "Oh," was her reply, "I haven't got my lesson to-day, and of course I must look pretty." There's fourteen-year-old female knowledge of human nature for you! Imagine a boy putting on his best jacket for such a purpose.

There must be discipline, that's certain; but, in my opinion, a man's head must be gray, not brown or black, if he would enforce it; his blood must be cold and sluggish, and his ear deaf to the charmer, charm she never so cunningly, or, certes, his magisterial chair will be set at naught. Don't I know! Answer me, thou now "Reverend" gentleman, who once kept me after school for a reprimand, and spent the precious moments rolling my curls over your fingers, while my comrade was bursting off her hooks and eyes as she peeped through the key-hole. Not that I uphold it, but every animal naturally fights with the weapons a good Providence has given it— and somehow or other I had found that out; though whether France was bounded south by Rhode Island or not was still a mystery that I was not in a hurry to solve.

Still, for all that, I pity a male teacher who is set to the impossible task of making girls "behave." I *should* pity them more, did I not know that they keep them in school about four or five hours longer than they ought. Did I not know what they know, but will persist practically in ignoring, that the fun has got to come out somehow, or turn to poison in the blood, and that if teachers won't give it whizzing time *out* of school, they must needs have it fly in their faces *in* school. I should pity them more, did I not, every day, see their pupils staggering home under a pile of stupidly written school-books, fit only to kindle the kitchen fire—thank goodness their little beaux sometimes save their arms from dislocation, by gallantly carrying them home for them. Do I approve of boy-beaux? Why not? Don't every rosebud draw its humming-bird? Did not God make them both for this harmless, innocent delight? You had *your* boy-beaux, madam; I had mine, by the score. Only teach your daughter to love you well enough to conceal nothing, however minute, from you; only show her that you have a heart, and don't want her to pluck out her's, and my word for it, no harm will come of her "boy-beaux." It is your repression that does the mischief—your ignoring your own youth and hers. The child who has leave to pluck the apple often leaves it untouched, *undesired*, on the tree.

Meantime our male teacher stands there, with his hands in his pockets, waiting to see what is to be done with *him*. Well, his pockets are the best place for his hands when he is keeping a girls' school; and with this advice I leave him, until he is sixty or so, when, if he chooses to open a girls' school, I promise him at least, that he will not go to sleep during the services.

Now let no conservative accuse me of upholding school rebellion. It is because I do *not* do this that I express my preference for women teachers, both principals and assistants, for girls; having an understanding of, and impervious to, girl witcheries, whom the little rogues know, having been girls themselves, can see through them, and for whom pretty looks or dresses will never answer instead of well-digested lessons.

A Safe Amusement.—All children are fond of animal pets, but it is so difficult to manage such pets in a city that no family can indulge its children's tastes in that respect to any great extent. No one can have watched the children in the Central Park, as they gaze at and linger over the bears and tigers and strange birds, without wishing that the little zoologists had a wider field and better opportunities for pursuing the study of natural history. There ought to be a permanent collection of animals and birds in New York, in some good situation, where children and young people could have ample opportunity, under proper restrictions, to indulge their natural taste for natural history. Every hour thus employed would be a safeguard against the myriad temptations to vice and idleness which pervade the city.

MY CALL ON "DEXTER."

THE other evening I went up to Fifty-sixth street to see the new stable. Mr. BONNER was out, but his horses were not. Now I didn't go to see them do their 2.40's, but to gaze at them artistically; and, of course, I wanted them to stand long enough for me to do it, which I believe is *not* their normal condition. I had a fancy, too, for inspecting them through the bars of their respective doors; for, you see, my nerves had been thrown a little out of gear by a huge blood-hound, that made for me as I was entering the stable-yard, but who, in consideration of my being a *Ledger* contributor, let me off easy in my boots.

Well, the first thing that struck my New England bred eyes was the perfect neatness and polish and beauty, of every inch of floor and ceiling in that stable. A place for everything, and everything in its place, and Mrs. BONNER nothing to do with it either! Shining harness, shining vehicles, big wheels and small seats, and nothing to hold on to—but the natty reins; a perfectly awful reflection to me, but then Mr. BONNER's arm *is* an arm! On the wall was something the size of a full moon; *red*, with a fanciful oak frame. It looked like a huge pincushion, and sure enough it was. Stuck full of wooden pins, to fasten the blankets of those horses round their wicked, strong necks. If it hadn't been for that blood-hound, which I heard sniffing round after me from the outside, I should have inspected it more carefully; but it was fastened to the wall near the door, and—well, I thought I'd pass on to see *Dexter*. My dear! your new seal-skin sack isn't softer, browner, nor more lovely than that creature's skin. And as to his tail, your latest "switch" is nothing to it! Mr. BONNER not being present to Rarey-fy him, he kicked out his hind leg at me in a very suggestive manner; so, with an Oh, gracious! I requested to have his door closed, for there was a glitter in his eye which was not at all Scriptural. Besides, I once flew through Harlem Lane behind him, and didn't get the color back into my lips for a week after. To compose myself I passed on to *Lantern*, the Grandpa of the stable, though I *have* known Grandparents rather frisky in my day. He was reposing on his laurels, and turned round his head to me as if to ask, Why don't you? Alas! I have yet to earn them, and unlike him, I have to pin on my own blanket, and comb my own hair, and buy my own shoes; that's why I don't, old *Lantern*.

Then I went to see *Startle*, as if I needed startling any more, when I had been muttering paternosters ever since I saw that horrid blood-hound. Well, *Startle* is a beauty, and he knew it too. Just like a piece of satin, with his tail sweeping the floor.

After I had looked at the whole ten, I said to myself, if ever a man earned *the right* to all these beautiful creatures, ROBERT BONNER has, from the time he first began to set types in a printing office, down, or rather *up*, to the present day. Every proud moment that he enjoys them, in or out of that handsome stable, he is fairly entitled to; and he is entitled to that blood-hound, and I wouldn't rob him of that for the wide world!

LADIES "WITHOUT AN OBJECT."—Ladies often give as a reason why they do not take exercise, "Oh, I don't like to go out without an object." Now nothing could prove more clearly their deplorable physical condition than this remark; since, to a well-organized frame, motion and fresh air are positive daily necessities; irrespective of any "object," save the cool play of the wind on the temples, and the healthful glow which follows a brisk walk. Medicine is a joke to it. No doctor, be his diploma ever so pretentious, could effect with simple means a more magical result. Considered only as "a beautifier," we marvel that the female portion of the community neglect it. A little chilliness in the air? A little sprinkling of rain? A high wind? An inability to display a fine dress? What puerile reasons for growing sallow, irritable, and sick.

THE POETRY OF WORK.

EXECUTIVE people have generally the reputation, from their opposites, of being ill-tempered people. Self-trained to the observance of the admirable old maxim, that "whatever is worth doing at all, is worth doing well," they are naturally disgusted with dawdling inefficiency and sloth in any shape. Chary of the precious flying moments, the most intolerable of vexations to them is to have their time trespassed upon, and wasted, in a million petty and unnecessary ways, by the stupidity or culpable thoughtlessness of those about them. Now what is called "an easy person," *i.e.*, a person who is not self-contained, on whose hands time hangs heavily, cannot be made to understand why a person of an opposite description need make a fuss about a few minutes. Why, "what is a few minutes?" they ask. Much, much in the course of a life-time to those who carefully husband them. Those "few minutes" may make all the difference between an educated and an uneducated person; between a man independent in his circumstances, and a man always under the grinding heel of want; all the difference between intelligence, thrift, and system on one hand, and ignorance, discomfort, and disaster on the other. Those "few minutes," carefully improved as they occur, have filled libraries with profound and choice volumes; those "few minutes," saved for mental cultivation, have enabled men, and women too, to shed over a life of toil a brightness which made even monotonous duty a delight. Such can ill afford to be robbed of them by those unable to appreciate their value. Like the infinitesimal gold scrapings of the mint, they may not be purloined, or carelessly brushed away by idle fingers; but conscientiously gathered up and accounted for; to be molten and stamped with thought, then distributed to bless mankind.

What a pleasure it is *to see anything perfectly done.* I never go "shopping" that I do not look on with admiration while the storekeeper so deftly does up my parcels. I believe no *woman* who has not acquired the professional shopkeeping touch, can do this decently. I like, too, to watch a group of men painting a house, provided the platform upon which they stand is so strong that my blood does not curdle lest their merry song should never be finished. With what a dexterous, careful, delicate touch they brighten up the unsightly wall; there is fascination to the looker-on in their skilful progress. Carpentering, too, I like; what pretty, silky, curled shavings they plane off; how many times, when a child, I placed them on my head for ringlets, have I mentally resolved to be a carpenter's wife, that I might always have plenty. How sure the stroke of their hammer upon the nail which a woman would bend, or break in pieces, beside jamming her fingers to a jelly. Mark the sturdy porter, too, as he tosses a huge "Saratoga trunk" lightly as a feather upon his back, and poising it, marches up uncounted stairs without tripping or bumping.

I like to see a strong man holding a fiery horse by a slight rein and a strong will. I like to see the oarsman in his red-shirt sleeves, pulling away over the sparkling water; I like to see the rough, red-faced omnibus driver making change, halting, gesticulating, hallooing to passers-by, all in the same breath. I like anything that is wide-awake and efficient, and if it be beautiful at the same time, so much the better. I like to see the cook toss eggs into a foam so nicely, with head turned the other way, watching pots, skillets, and frying-pans, and at the same time giving orders to half a dozen subordinates. I like to see a milliner twist a ribbon into a thousand fanciful shapes while talking, or selecting a rose from one box, a green spray from another, then a spear of wheat, a daisy and a poppy, twine them together with an artist's taste and touch. I like to see the dressmaker fit the glossy silk to the curve of limbs as soft as the silky fabric. I like to see the flushed pressman sliding the damp newspapers from the "form" without a flaw or a wrinkle. I like to see a mother strip her little, tender babe, and bathe its fragile limbs with that wonderful delicacy of touch which mothers only know, singing, caressing, patting, and soothing, till the lovely task is done. I like to see those little imps of newsboys running indiscriminately between the legs of man and beast, yelling out their precocious wisdom about "accidents and arrivals;" dodging under carts, and coming out safe in wind and limb; thriving, in spite of dirt and rags, to turn up some day, ten to one, in a big marble store up town, as bookseller or publisher.

I am not at all sure, now that blessed chloroform is discovered by which my faith in the predicted millennium has had a most vigorous quickening (why *don't* they build a statue to the discoverer?) that I could not look on admiringly while the surgeon's knife wound amid veins and arteries with almost omnipotent skill, his patient lying calm as a sleeping infant the while.

And now the thought comes over me with overwhelming force, how strange that we, who so adore strength, power, beauty, and perfection, should be content with its circumscribed *human* progress; never look for it, never worship it, where it is limitless, unchangeable, unfettered by selfishness, caprice, or injustice. Alas! till we learn this, we shall, vine-like, throw out our tendrils to the mercy of every passing breeze, with nothing sure to twine around or cling to.

CAN'T KEEP A HOTEL.

A MAN who has no call to keep a hotel had better not try it, unless he can be certain that the horizon of his guests has always been bounded by the village hay-scales. Noble scenery is a fine thing; but mountain, nor lake, nor river, was ever enjoyable in company with an empty stomach, or one which is in the talons of the fiend, *indigestion*. To come to one's meal with loathing, and eat because we must, or starve, and then hurry from grease and saleratus as soon as possible, is not the best receipt a landlord can use to insure a good class of customers for another season. He may think it of no consequence that his garden, if he have one, be as full of nettles as of flowers; that the walks have more pig-weed than gravel in them; that his out-buildings are more conspicuous than any other object both to the eye and nose; and that the grass-plats about the house are strewn with perpetual rags, paper, and old boots, which a fervid August sun is not generally inclined to mitigate.

He may "take things easy" when his guests, having engaged the hotel-carriage and horses for a ride are still standing on the piazza waiting half an hour past the time; and when, on its dilatory appearance, the harness is found giving out at the last minute, having been patched and repatched in a slovenly manner on uncounted previous rides; while the golden sunset, on which his guests had reckoned, is spent in a fruitless search for *that* hammer and *thóse* nails, which elude all pursuit. He may think it good policy to keep his *regular* boarders waiting for their meals an hour past the appointed time, while hungry children fret for sustenance, because newcomers will *then* appear, and this stratagem will save the trouble of preparing *two* meals. He may do all that if he will; but he must remember that every disgusted guest who leaves his establishment will prevent many from coming to it; and that with such a short-sighted policy he will soon find "his occupation gone."

Keeping a hotel is a *gift*, as much as poetry, or sculpture, or painting. I might name men whose hotels have attained perfection under their wise, cleanly, and systematic ordering; but perfect as they are, I, for one, am not employed to advertise them over the length and breadth of the land in the New York *Ledger*. Suffice it to say, that I have slept on their lovely beds, and had four towels a day to wash my hands on. That I had a roomy wardrobe for such of my clothes as I desired to set free from my trunk. That the looking-glass was *not* located in the *darkest* corner of the room, or placed so high that I had to stand on tip-toe, or so low that I had to get on my knees to myself. That the coffee was not made of split peas. That the fried potatoes even an angel like me might eat. That the meats were cooked in a Christian manner, and the bread guiltless of any abominable "Sal"—anything. That the pastry, which I never touch, *looked* good for those who like it; and that the ale—oh! the ale was "divine." That in the spots where cleanliness might not be looked for, there it reigned. That no chambermaid came with scraping broom against my door, at daylight, to rouse me from my slumbers, and shuffle and flirt with the boot-and-shoe collectors at the different doors. That no "pictures" of ambitious artists upon the walls gave me the nightmare. And, oh! more—far more than this, that the well-mannered landlord never made a menagerie—show—of any "lion," or lioness, in his house, by labelling the same, on the instant of their appearance, in dining-hall or parlor, for the unwinking stare of the curious.

Of course, such a house needs money as well as an artist-master to carry it on. Of course, guests who register their names there, must foot the cost of all this outlay on their bills.

One can buy a bonnet at a pawn-shop, if one is satisfied only with cheapness; but the dainty, artistic fingers, which blend colors and fabrics with the lightness and brightness of inspiration, cannot be expected to sell so much talent at a pawnbroker's price.

Your physician, who stays in your house only five minutes, charges you, perhaps, fifteen dollars. You stare wildly at the amount; but you do not take into account the human bodies he has overhauled, and the libraries and lectures he has mastered to arrive at the knowledge which he has concentrated for your benefit in that brief five minutes. In homely phrase, "you pays your money and you takes your choice." Or, "he is a good-natured man, but he can't keep a hotel," nor will people stay with him long, though Paradise lies out-doors.

WOMEN LOVERS.—Perhaps you don't know it, but there are women that fall in love with each other. Woe be to the unfortunate she who *does the courting!* All the cussedness of ingenuity peculiar to the sex is employed by "the other party" in tormenting her. She will flirt with women by the score who are brighter and handsomer than her victim. She will call on them oftener. She will praise their best bonnet, and go into ecstasies over their dresses. She will write them more pink notes, and wear their "tin types;" and when despair has culminated, and sore-hearted Araminta takes to her bed in consequence, then only will this conquering she, step off her pedestal to pick up her dead and wounded. But then women must keep their hand in. Practice makes perfect.

NEW CLOTHES.

IT is curious with what different eyes human beings look upon new clothes, at different stages of existence. Youth, which least needs these auxiliaries, is generally the most clamorous for incessant change. No discomfort in the way of perpetual guardianship over their freshness; no uncomfortable sense of their weight or pressure on the limbs, is heeded, so that the craving for them is satisfied. Nor is there any sex to this foible. Young men are quite as apt to be caught tripping in this regard as their sisters. The new coat may squeeze; the new collar may strangle; the new boots may pinch; the new hat may leave its red mark on the throbbing forehead, but perish the thought of not wearing either! The self-immolation which is undergone in this way finds no mention in "Fox's Book of Martyrs;" but its silent, tearless, uncomplaining heroism exists none the less for all that. From the days when our foremothers had their heads built up in turrets by the hurried hair-dresser, the night previous to some great festive occasion, and sat bolstered upright in bed all night, for fear of tumbling them—down to the present day of ladies' "hair-crimpers," human nature has held its own in this respect.

Middle age, with few exceptions, looks upon new clothes with abated interest. Old clothes, like old customs, fit easy. *Comfort*, anyhow, says middle age—appearances as the gods please; so new shoes lie on the shelf unworn for weeks, for fear of stiff heels or squeaky soles; and new clothes look and feel so spick-and-span and glossy, that middle age can no more say or do a natural thing in them, than the boy could spell right " before he had got the hang of the new school-house; " middle age resents this petty, fretting intrusion on its much-loved quiet. It is irritable, till new clothes begin to *feel* easy, which is not generally the case till some seam grows threadbare, or some treacherous gap horrifies the easy wearer with renewed visions of innovating fashions and fabrics.

Now this is very natural and very well, too, to a certain extent; but middle age sometimes forgets that something is due to affectionate young eyes, which take a proper pride in seeing " father " or " mother " neatly and becomingly dressed, according to their age and station in life. Roses and snow, of course, nobody looks for; but the trim evergreen shows well, even beside a snow-bank; and nature herself hangs glistening pendants of icicles from the glossy leaves of the ivy.

It is a harrowing reflection how much money is "sunk" every day in new clothes, in which the blissfully unconscious wearers look none the better, but rather the worse. Still, if everybody had good taste in this matter, there would be no foil to the well-dressed; and I am afraid the heartless dry-goods merchants care little whether blondes dress in orange color, or brunettes in sky-blue, so that their bills are paid.

But new clothes for the "baby." Ah! that is something worth while. I ask you, did love ever find fabric soft enough, or nice enough, or pretty enough, for "*the baby*"? Fathers and mothers may make as virtuously economical resolutions as they please; but why, if they mean to carry them out, do they linger at the shop-window where that dainty little satin bonnet stares them innocently in the face, with that pert little rosette, cocked upon one side, that "would look so cunning on baby." Why do they contemplate the rows of bright little red-prunella boots, or the embroidered little sacques and frocks? Why don't they cross right over and travel home out of the way of temptation? Surely, no pink could rival the rose of baby's cheek; no crimson the coral of its lips; no blue the sapphire of its eyes. For all that, out comes the purse and home goes the bonnet, or cloak, or frock. Just as if shopkeepers didn't know that babies will keep on being born, and born pretty; and that fathers and mothers are, and will be, their happy slaves all the world over to the end of time!

HOW I READ THE MORNING PAPERS.

IF there is a time when I sigh for the "Cave of Adullam," whatever that may be, it is when, my coffee swallowed, my fingers clutch my precious, morning papers, for a blessed, quiet read.

I just begin an editorial, which requires a little thinking, when up comes Biddy with "Ma'am, there's a hole in the *biler*." The "biler" settled, I go back to the place indicated by my forefinger, where the Editor was saying "that Congress—" when somebody upsets the coffee-pot in an attempt to burlesque last night's public performance. The coffee-pot set right end up, and the coffee pond drained off the table-cloth, I return again to my beloved editorial;—when Biddy again appears with "Ma'am, the man has come to mend the door-handle as is broke." That nuisance disposed of, I take my paper and retreat in self-defence to the top of the house, and commence to read again, "that Congress—" when I am interrupted with loud shouts of "Where's mother? Mother? where are you?" I disdain to answer. "Mother?" In despair, I cry, in tragic tones, "Well, what *is* it?" "A poor soldier is at the door with pictures at thirty cents apiece, and he has but one arm." "Well, I have but one life—but for mercy's sake take his pictures, and don't let in anything else, man, woman, or child, till I read my paper through." I begin again: "If Congress—" when Biddy, who is making the bed in the next room, begins howling "Swate Ireland is the land for me." I get up and very mildly request—in view of a possible visit to an Intelligence Office—that she will oblige me by deferring her concert till I get through my morning paper. Then I begin again: "If Congress—" when up comes paterfamilias to know if it is to be beef, or chicken, or veal, that he is to order at market for that day's dinner. "Possum, if you like," I mutter, with both fingers on my ears, as I commence again, "If Congress—" Paterfamilias laughs and retreats, exclaiming, "Shadrachs! vot a womansh!" and I finish "Congress," and begin on the book reviews. A knock on the door. "Six letters, ma'am." I open them. Three for an "autograph," with the privilege of finding my own envelope and stamp, and mailing it afterward. One with a request for me to furnish a speedy "composition" to save a school-boy at a dead-lock of ideas from impending suicide. One from a man who has made a new kind of polish for the legs of tables and chairs, and wants me to write an article about it in the *Ledger*, and send him an early copy of the same. One from a girl "who never in her life owned a dress bonnet," and would like, with my assistance, to experience that refreshing and novel sensation.

I begin again my postponed list of "book reviews;" when in comes paterfamilias to know "if I haven't yet done with that paper." That's the last ounce on the camel's back! Mind you, *he* has just read *his* morning paper through, and it contains a different stripe of politics from mine, I can tell you that. Read it in *peace*, too—with his legs on the mantel, smoking his beloved pipe. Read it up and down; backwards and forwards; inside out, and upside down; and disembowelled every shade of meaning from live and dead subjects; and then coolly inquires of me—me, with my hair on end in the vain effort to retain any ideas through all these interruptions—"if I haven't *yet* done with that paper?" Oh, it's *too* much! I sit down opposite him. I explain how I never get a chance to finish anything except himself. I tell him my life is all fragments. I ask him, with moist eyes, if he knows how the price of board ranges at the different Lunatic Asylums. What is his unfeeling answer? "Hadn't I better take some other hour in the day to read the papers?"

Isn't that just like a man?

Has not bother and worry "all seasons for its own," as far as women are concerned? Would it make any difference what "hour in the day" I took to read the papers? *Can* women *ever* have any system about anything, while a Biddy or a male creature exists on the face of the earth to tangle up things? Have I not all my life been striving and struggling for that "order" which my copy-book told me in my youth "was Heaven's first law"? And is it my fault if "chaos," which I hate, is my "unwilling portion"?

I just propounded to paterfamilias these vital questions. With eyes far off on distant, and untried, and possible fields of literature, he absently replies: "Well, as you say, Fanny, I shouldn't wonder if it *does* rain to-day." Great heavens!

SMOKING BABIES.—It would not be amiss to call the attention of parents and school-teachers to the fact that every morning, lads from seven years old to twelve may be seen, satchel in hand, *smoking* on their way to school. Surely, between the parents and the teachers, some remedy should immediately be devised to prevent this enormous tax upon the vitality of youth. A great deal has very properly been written and spoken upon the mismanagement of young girls who have not yet reached their teens. Why not extend this philanthropic solicitude to their brothers? Is it because smoking fathers, being themselves slaves to this vile habit, have not the face to ask their sons to practise a self-denial, of which their own manhood is incapable?

BETTY'S SOLILOQUY.

HARD to live out? Well, that's just as you choose to take it. Some folks have no faculty at getting along in this world. My name is Easy, and my nature is ditto. When I go to a place I always say "yes" to everything they ask me. I never make an objection to doing anything; of course, my mistress likes that; as to really doing all I promise to do, leave me alone to manage that, with as innocent a face as the baby I take care of. Now, for instance, suppose she sends me up into the nursery to get the child asleep. It is tiresome work; there's a great deal of coaxing, and twisting, and wriggling, and rocking, and singing to be done, before that can be brought about; and it tires me, and I don't like it. But of course I reply, "Certainly, ma'am," when she bids me, and I take the child upstairs. Then I sit down with it; and just hold it in some uncomfortable position so that it will cry loud enough to fret its mamma. Then she bears it awhile, thinking baby will stop by and by; but baby somehow *don't* stop. Then she comes up and says to me, "Betty what do you think *can* ail baby!" And I kiss it and hold it up to my face, and say, "Poor little dear, I am afraid it has a bad stomach ache; it won't be easy—anyhow I try;"

and then she says, " Well, I'll take it awhile, Betty, and see if I can't soothe it asleep;" and I say, " Oh no, ma'am, it is a pity you should tire yourself with the child;" and she seeing me so willing, just takes it—don't you see? *That's* the way to do. There's no use in *fighting* one's way through the world, when a little cunning answers just as well. Well, then my mistress likes baby to go out of doors a great deal. Now, as a general thing, I never engage to live with a lady who don't keep her own carriage, on that account. It's very nice to be sent out in a carriage with the baby, for an airing, with John, the coachman, particularly when John is agreeable, which is sometimes the case. It makes a body feel like somebody to say, " John, you may drive here, or, John, you may drive there." But of course one cannot always get a place to one's mind; and so when my mistress uses her feet instead of a carriage, she needn't think that I shall do it any more than I can possibly help. So when she tells me to take baby out, I say, " Yes'em," as I always do, respectfully, I hope—and out I go, and make for the first kitchen where I have a pleasant acquaintance, and baby can wait till we get through our gossip, which is not very soon. Of course, I never take a little tell-tale of an older child with me on such occasions. I tell mistress I'm so afraid of its getting run over, or something, while I'm minding baby. Then as to my " privileges," I hope I know enough to have one of my friends sick or dead if I want an evening out. There can't anything be said against that, you know, if one is only judicious enough not to have it happen *too* often. Sometimes I come across a mistress who is too keen for me. Now I never like to live with a lady who has gray eyes; in that case we have a mutual inclination to part, of course; but as a general thing, I find my way of managing "*fust-rate*," because I give no "impudence," you see, which is what most ladies are so touchy about. As to "conscience," humph! where are *their* "consciences," I'd like to know? It is a poor rule that won't work both ways. I should be worn to a skeleton if I kept a conscience.

BRIDAL PRESENTS.—If brides could only hear the conversations that are held over the "bridal presents" by the givers! Their weary yawns while pondering how much *must* be expended, and how little *may;* and wishing heartily the whole system were exploded, in favor of their pockets. If brides could hear this, they would quietly and with dignity announce, "No presents received," even without any reservations as to relationship. It is of no use talking of the "good old days," we suppose; as well might one ask a confirmed epicure to adjure his Cayenne, and highly spiced diet for plain, wholesome, nutritious food; so, with a passing sigh for the days when sentiment, modesty, and economy had not yet gone out of fashion, we give it up.

MY DREADFUL BUMP OF ORDER.

I HAVE just been reading a "sweet" article, headed "Coming Home After the Summer Vacation," in which the writer looks through his "glory spectacles" upon the delights of plenty of elbow-room in the dear old house; good fare, and one's little personal hourly comforts generally. *All very well.* But what of the carpets to be shaken and steamed, or the new ones to be made? What of the painting and whitewashing, and cleaning out of cellars and closets? What of the new kitchen-range, and the new oilcloth for the floor? What of the plumbing and roof painting? What of the winter's coal to get in, which *paterfamilias* always "forgets" to order till the fall house-cleaning is done? What of upholsterers and painters and plumbers, who begin a job, and finish it whenever the gods will? What of crisp, sunny, lovely autumn mornings spent in the delightful atmosphere of an "Intelligence Office" six feet by eight, while *answering* the following questions: "Any children in the family? Have you an English basement? Have you a servant's parlor? Do you put out your washing? Does your cook wash the dishes? Do you use such and such a kitchen-range?" All of which questions, answered in the affirmative, giving you the inestimable boon of a poor cook, at sixteen, eighteen, or twenty dollars a month, with liberty to have her "cousins" visit her at will. After that comes your waitress, and if you want to preserve your senses you had better end there, without encumbering yourself with more "help."

There is nothing said about all *this* in the "sweet" article alluded to, called "Coming Home After the Summer Vacation." I didn't see anything in it either about the children's dilapidated wardrobe, to be then replenished, with dress-makers knee-deep in engagements, and "Furnishing Stores for Children's Outfits," containing only lace and ruffles, to wear to school. As to your own wardrobe, if you are possessed of a black silk, or alpaca, or Cashmere walking-suit, blessed are you among women—for then you at least are always presentable in public.

Well, after all this, there is a chance that the new cook, not admiring the new waitress, whom *you* happen to like, may conclude to quarrel her off, in order to fill the vacancy with a raw "cousin" just from shipboard: and directly, when you think the family machine is at last oiled, and in motion for the winter, and you are taking breath upon that idea, in comes the irate waitress, and you are "to choose, ma'am, if you please, between me and the cook, for indeed the house will not hold both of us," and so on, and so forth.

Here most lady housekeepers come to the end of their calamities. But suppose you help to earn the family bread and butter as a writer? Then may the gods send you patience, or a new set of nerves and muscles and brains! May the gods preserve you from reading yourself the crudities you give to the public for base lucre! May the gods sustain you under the torturing reflection, how much better literary work you know yourself to be capable of, had you only a fair chance at your freshest moments, and could you inaugurate that "system" in your household to which Intelligence Offices are an insurmountable obstacle; which you, New England born and bred, adore and understand, but yet can never bring about with any "increase of wages," or even personal supervision; not, at least, while the demand for household servants is always greater than the supply, and they can make their own terms, and exhaust your vitality much faster than they can their own vocabulary of abuse.

Knowing thoroughly *this* side of "Coming Home After the Summer Vacation," I perused the article with this heading, with the corners of my mouth slightly drawn down, and the end of my nose slightly turned up. And if any lady remarks, in reply, that *she* "admires housekeeping in all its details," I can only say, that I have observed that slack housekeepers generally do, as their topsy-turvy cupboards bear witness. And I also unhesitatingly affirm that no thorough housekeeper, in the present day of incompetent, careless servants, who desires time for anything else save the hourly needs of the body, can conscientiously make such assertion; although, as wife and mistress, she may not at the same time refuse to meet the consequent exhaustive demands upon her vitality; that is, so long as she can possibly bear the strain.

It is a trying thing to have the bump of order too fully developed. Now I have trotted across this room twenty times to pick up little bits of thread and shining pins, that offended my eye, upon this floor. I positively couldn't write till I had done it. Then that vase was placed a little awry when the room was dusted, and I had to get up and settle its latitude and longitude. The hearth, too, had some ashes upon it, and there was a shawl on the sofa that should have been in the closet. Then there was an ink-spot on my thumb that had to be removed, and my desk had a speck or two of dust on the corner. All these things bothered me; and then I fell thinking whether it were not, after all, better not to have quite so sharp an eye for these things; that perhaps editors were right who had their office windows so thickly crusted with dirt that they could not tell whether it were a rainy or a sunshiny day from indoor observation. That perhaps they were right in heaping breast-high upon their office desks papers, books, MSS., letters, pencils, pens, gloves, hats, and cigar-stumps, varied with engravings and dirty pocket-handkerchiefs. Perhaps they were right in never sweeping their floors, and leaving it to their visitors to dust their chairs with their clothes.

Really it is quite a question with me this morning, whether the bump of order is not a nuisance, even to a woman. Now at any chance table where I may lunch, I have regularly to re-locate the cups, saucers, and dishes, before I begin, placing them where their geographical relation will be most harmonious. If the folds in the table-cloth run the wrong way, I assure you I am quite miserable; and a missing stopper to the vinegar cruet drives me to despair. Then I endeavor so to regulate my bureau drawers and closets that a visit to them in the darkest night, without a light, for any article, would be eminently successful. Till, "*Now, who has been here,*" has come to be a miserable joke against me, by the happy creatures who cannot comprehend, that to misplace my gloves, or handkerchiefs, or ribbons, or veil, is to cause my too susceptible heart an exquisite anguish, beside wasting my precious time in fruitless hunts for the same.

Then I may be very tired when I return at twelve o'clock at night from some visit or place of amusement; but no amount of reasoning could avail to get me to bed till my bonnet, cloak, and dress were put away in their appropriate places. I am sorry to confess that unless I did this, visions of Betty and a broom in possible connection with them, the next morning, would quite interfere with my slumbers. You may laugh at all this; but 'tis I who would laugh at *you* in the morning, when you are spending the best hours of the day in flying distractedly round for some missing article which you cannot do without, and which, of course, *nobody has seen*. If "Order is Heaven's first law," as my school copy-book used to assert, my initiatory carefulness here below may not be, after all, without its value. Still, I do not forget that there was once a Martha who was rebuked for "being careful and troubled about many things."

But stay a bit: can you tell me *why*, when one's room is what they call "put to rights," the table which has a drawer in it should always be so left by Bridget that the drawer side faces the wall? Or why, when a basin of water is in use, to cleanse spots from paint, it should always be placed near the door, that the first comer may enjoy an impromptu foot-bath? Why, in moving a vase, or any other fragile article, it is always so located, that breakage is inevitable? Why should dust-pans be left in dark entries, or stairways, to the sudden precipitation of some unsuspecting victim? Why, when a broom is off duty, should it be "stood up" where the handle is sure to make thumping acquaintance with one's nose? Why should soiled towels be abstracted, before replacing them with fresh ones, and you left to make the harrowing discovery with dripping finger-ends? Oh! tell me why need your bonnet be put in the coal-scuttle, and your muddy gaiter-boots in the bandbox? Why should your "honey-soap" be used to wash the hearth? Why, when you beseech that blankets, and sheets, and coverlets, should be tucked harmoniously in at the bottom of the bed, should your toes make unwilling acquaintance, every night, with the cold foot-board? Why, when you request that a door should be kept shut, is it always left wide open? and why, when you are in a gasping condition, should it be carefully closed, spite of repeated remonstrance?

Gentle Shepherd, tell me, are pigs and Bridgets *the only* creatures whom heaven and earth can't stop from going east, if you desire them to go west? And the Shepherd answers—*Man*.

MOTHERS OF MANY CHILDREN.—"Ponder every subject with careful attention, if you wish to acquire knowledge." What is then to be the mental status of that mother who has a *perpetual* baby in her arms, and only time to "ponder" that baby, so weary is her body with its "ponder"-osity? Where is the Solomon to answer this question? Baby knowledge she may indeed have; but the baby will grow up by and by, and how is she to acquire "knowledge" under such circumstances, and be a fit intellectual companion for it then? That's what some people want to know, when little brothers and sisters tread so fast on each other's heels, that the mother has scarcely breathing time between.

"EVERY FAMILY SHOULD HAVE IT."

ONE actually gasps for breath in crowded, closetless New York to read this frequent newspaper announcement, "Every family should have it." Modern times having abolished the "garret of our forefathers with its all-embracing omnium-gatherum eaves," the prospect of dire confusion is terrible if "every family" does not turn a deaf ear to these disinterested caterers for their benefit. Alas! for that old blessed garret, the standing curiosity shop for the youngsters of a rainy or a holiday afternoon; that mausoleum of "notions" cast aside by our venerated ancestors, who undoubtedly had their little follies like their descendants. Old boxes, old tins, old baskets, old hats, old bonnets, old school-books, old bottles, did not then, as now, marshal themselves on the sidewalks, in company with coal cinders, to the disgust of every pedestrian, waiting the snail-like operations of the dirt-man, who is off duty six days out of the seven, and spills half he carries away at that, besides knocking the bottom out of every barrel when, having essayed to disembowel it, he jerks it off one wheel of his cart to the sidewalk. One needs to go to Boston or to Philadelphia occasionally to air one's nostrils and temper after it. After this, to talk of more things, each day, that "every family must have," is enough to drive one to a druggist's for speedy oblivion. What a blessing to these public and disinterested philanthropists, of "every family," are gullible housekeepers and matrons who, though cheated and bamboozled seventy times seven, are still on hand for the latest sham—"improvement." Credulous souls! How do their husbands count over to them on warning marital fingers the dismal amount thus uselessly expended! Not that *they themselves* do not, and have not, erred in the same way; but who is going to have the superhuman courage to tell these sinless beings so? But after all, far be it from me to say that there are not many things that "every family must have;" and one of these is a baby. Not that *they* too are not occasionally dumped unceremoniously and heartlessly on the sidewalk; but that don't alter the fact, that a house without a baby is no house at all. Another thing that "every family must have," is a Doctor; also a Minister. Who ever heard of a woman without these two confidential friends—what would become of her if she couldn't make a good cup of tea for the latter, and tell the other her real and imaginary aches? And if she knows anything, can't she always choose her own sanitary prescriptions, all the same as if there were no diploma in her Doctor's pocket?

I will not stop to inquire whether this advertisement-heading is a disinterested one, or whether they who deal in such things are conversant with the respective sizes of our houses, or families, or both; or whether new complications of pots and pans, and tea-kettles, and gridirons, and egg-beaters, and clothes-wringers, and the like, will only wring to utter extinction the already muddled heads of our unscientific "help" and the depleted purses of housekeepers, consequent upon their unthrift. We only wish to remind these disinterested shopkeepers, who would fain take in verdant housekeepers, that houses nowadays are mainly constructed without garrets, without cellars, without closets, without any lumber place whatsoever, where the wrecks of these articles "that no family can do without," can be ultimately stranded. Their wares are, to be honest, often tempting enough to look at; beautiful in their shining freshness, and deliciously suggestive of good roasts and stews and broils—*awfully* suggestive of the latter!—but " terrible as an army with banners," when contemplating " Intelligence offices "; though why " *intelligence*," when anything *but* that is to be had there, I have heretofore failed to see.

Another question I would ask these disinterested persons who have so many "articles no family can do without:" Did they ever hear of the *First of May?* Have they a realizing sense of what it is to "move"? Will they tell us, when moving carts are already bursting with "the things no family can do without," and the sidewalk refuses to receive the remainder, and the new tenant won't have them at any price, and you are wild with despair that it is impossible for you to be divorced from them—will they tell us, at that halcyon moment, if they really contemplated, in the affluence of their desires to furnish our houses, that they might be the means of sending us to a lunatic asylum?

Beggars are useful at such times, if they only wouldn't sort out the horrid heap of broken and disabled things that "the family can" *now* do very well "without," directly in the path of the moving carts, and before your afflicted eyes, that are quite ready to close on all things here below, so intense is your disgust of them.

The words "do without" convey to me a very different meaning now than of yore. A new dumping-ground must be invented in New York before *I* patronize any more inventions. I'm for condensing instead of expanding things, till our city masters find time to attend to that. Nobody need ring my door-bell with "patent" anything, while it is so patent that there is no vacant space in Manhattan for anything new under the sun. My nature is not conservative; but one can't be pushed into the East river, when it is so full of the "things that no family can do without," that there is not room enough left there even to sink.

GETTING TO RIGHTS.

THERE! I breathe again! The household is at last wound up—carpets down, house-cleaning accomplished; all the "pretties" located in the most effective places; my flowers and ivies luxuriant; my desk newly fitted up; everything thriving save myself; but that's no consequence, I suppose. My play-day is over, and now I must buckle down to realities. Still one's home *is* lovely after the jar of the creaking machinery used in getting it in order has ceased. Your own chair, just fitted to your weary back; your own convenient dressing-room and glass, with all your little duds close to your hand; gas, instead of kerosene; bell-wires ready to your hand, instead of having to descend stairs and do your own errands; food cooked your own way, and just when you want it; and over and above all, to be able to say what shall, and what shall not, be *inside* your front door. May the gods make us thankful so far! But if I *could* get a breath of dear Newport now, before I buckle down to work; if I could have just *one* drive more in my horse and phaeton round the "ocean road," and smell the good salt breeze, and see the crisp white foam of the dashing waves, I think it would quite set me up for the winter campaign. As to my horse, I know he wants me as much as I do him. I don't think he has made much, in exchanging my free and go-easy "chirrup" for the lash of the whip. I wish I were a man, and then I could drive here in the city; but I ain't, you see, and so I shall have to get the snarl out of my tired nerves some other way.

Let us change the subject. Is it not funny how a man will go on inspecting your efforts to get a house to rights? Is it not funny how he never can tell how "a thing is going to look," till every accessory is perfected? Now he says, "What made you choose that dull carpet, nobody can tell." You reply, "Because it is capable of such brilliant contrasts in color." He shakes his head, having no imagination to help him out, and thinks it "a blunder." You smile serenely, knowing your ground, and bide your time, while he croaks. By and by, some day, when he has gone out, the little bits of color are added by you, here and there: a bright vase, or a cushion, or a stand of flowers, or the color of a mat judiciously chosen; and my gentleman walks in, and says, "Why, who would have thought it? it is really lovely!" That, of course, is only setting himself down for a goose; but when is ever a man anything else, when he attempts to criticise a woman's housekeeping in any of its departments? You despise his encomiums now, and with nose in air, walk round among your flowers and pretties, as if to say, "In future, sir, confine yourself to Gradgrind matters that you understand, and leave the decorative part of your existence to one who—Hem!"

I ache from head to foot with my herculean efforts to bring things in this house to a bright New England focus. But I am not sorry, because I can now put to rout some articles lately written, by a very bright woman too, on "the inexactness of hired women's work, as compared to the fidelity and exactness of hired men's work." I am happy to state, that after my new parlor carpets were nailed down, by *men* too, I discovered several little blocks of wood and other nuisances underneath, which should have been first removed; thus perilling the future wear of my pretty new carpet. I am happy to state too, that the papering done by men was not to my mind, or *according to my order*, and had to be done over again. I rejoice to say that my window-shades are not yet forthcoming, according to a *man's* promise; and that it was only by personal supervision that my cellar was thoroughly cleansed by a *man*, as he agreed it should be. In short, I don't want to hear any more on the "*exactness* of man's work," since he can fib, and slight things, with an adroitness worthy of a woman, and I am sure I couldn't put the case any stronger.

Now I am going to fold my hands and be comfortable. I can't have my horse this winter, and so I sha'n't sigh any more for *him;* but if I live till the spring, that horse, or some other, has got to help me get rid of this world's cares and perplexities every blessed sunny afternoon. Let us trust that he is fattening up on oats paid and provided for in the stable of some philanthropist unknown to me. I have had so much of the *details* lately, that I shall be quite satisfied with *results* without inquiring further.

I wish I were a voter: I would vote for the officials who would take a little interest in the household ash-barrel. It may be too much to ask that the McGormicks, and McCormicks, and O'Flahertys, who are paid for emptying these utensils—when it don't rain, and when they don't forget it—should not empty the contents on the pavement, and then half shovel them up, to save themselves the exertion of lifting the barrels, which they always throw down upon their sides, to roll wheresoever the gods or idle boys will. It may be too much to ask that they should amend their ways in these particulars; but were every lady housekeeper a voter, as, thank Providence, they are sure to be some day or other, these gentlemen would either have to toe the mark, or be run over by the new wheel of progress.

Meantime, it is of little use for Bridget to sweep the sidewalk, or keep the gutter free, as she often pathetically remarks to me, when she goes forth to perform this matutinal duty. Now, as the tools used in my profession keep sharper and freer from rust, in the air of Manhattan, than elsewhere, I cannot be expected to vacate for the dry-dirt-man. The only alternative that I know of is, that *he* shall vacate for me, and make room for more executive officials. That's logic, if it is feminine. In short, I want those men to take a little journey somewhere—I'm not particular where, so that they don't come back.

It grows clearer to me, every day, as I observe these one-horse arrangements, why women are not allowed to vote: there would be little margin then for all this cheating, this pocketing of salaries without an equivalent. The sidewalks, gutters, streets would be as clean as a parlor floor. No old boxes, or kegs, or boots and shoes, past their prime, would challenge our eyes, or our noses. The drinking-places would be disgorged of husbands, fathers, lovers, and brothers; also the billiard and gambling saloons. In short, the broom of reform would raise such a dust in the eyes of the *how-not-to-do-its*, that, when their vision was restored, they would ask, like the old woman whose skirts were curtailed while taking her nap, if "this be I?"

Meantime I wait—not patiently—for this millennium. It galls me—this dirt and thriftlessness—more in the Autumn than at any other time. In the Spring it is sufficiently odious; but then one is on the wing for the country, and that hope buoys a housekeeper under it. In the Winter the friendly, pure white snow comes, with its heavenly mantle of charity, to cover it sometimes. But who or what shall comfort the housekeeper in the lingering, golden days of the Indian Summer, when fresh from the pure air of the country, and the brilliant foliage of the valleys, and the lovely shadows on the hillsides, she is doomed to see, to smell, to breathe whatever of pollution and unthrift our city fathers choose, without the power to cast the vote that shall give us a clean city?

Meantime, as I say, I wait—*not* patiently—for that desired millennium; and shall continue, with a touching faith in it, to keep flowering plants in my windows, and in other ways to signify, to the passer-by, that dirt and unsightliness, and bad odors, are not and never have been, the normal condition of *woman*.

OUR MORNING MEAL.—Breakfast should be the most enlivening meal of the whole day, for then we are to be nerved for another day's duties and cares, and perhaps for great sorrows also. Let there be no exciting argument, from which personalities may crop out, around the breakfast table. Let there be, if possible, only pleasant topics, and affectionate salutations, that all may go forth their separate ways with sweet, peaceful memories of each other; for some foot may never again cross the family threshold, some eye never witness another day's dawning. This thought, if the busy world were not so clamorous as to stifle it, would often arrest the impatient, fretful words that pain so many tender hearts.

MODERN MARTYRS.

FOX'S cheerful "Book of Martyrs" strikes us as incomplete. He tells, to be sure, of people who have been roasted alive, cut up, torn limb from limb, disembowelled, and suffered various other trifling annoyances of that kind; but though I have perused it carefully, I see no mention of the unhappy wretch who, coming home at twelve o'clock at night, with frozen fingers, gropes round his room, bumping his nose, and extinguishing his eyes, in the vain search for his match-box, the latitude and longitude of which some dastardly miscreant has changed. Nor do I see any mention of him who, having washed his hands nicely, looketh in vain for a towel, where a towel *should* be, while little rivulets of water run up his shirt-sleeves or drip from his extended finger-tips. No allusion either is made to her who, sitting down to her time-honored portfolio, misseth one sheet of MS. which somebody has fluttered out, and straightway gone his heedless way. Nor yet of the unhappy owner of a pen, whose pace answers only to one hand, and whose nib has been tampered with by some idle scribbler, in multiplying the name of "Laura," or "Matilda," to an indefinite extent, over a sheet of paper as blank as his mind. I see no mention of her who, sitting down to write, is made frantic by the everlasting grind of a handorgan beneath the window; that performer's welcome retreat being followed by a shaky old man with a wheezy flute, or the more horrible bagpipe performance, compared with which the shrieks of twenty cur-tailed cats were heaven's own music. I have not noticed any mention of her who, giving her husband a letter to drop into the post, finds the same a month afterwards in the pocket of a vest, which he tosses her to mend. I see no mention of the lady-victims of owners of shops, three miles long, who have always "*just the article you want*" at the very farthest extremity of the store; and whom they lure to traverse that distance only to find something in the *shopman's* view "infinitely superior," but about as near the article wanted as is the North to the South pole. No mention either is made of the gentleman with a bran new coat, who takes the last seat in the car, next a child fond of wriggling, with a piece of soft gingerbread or a moist stick of candy in its uncertain gripe. Nor is any allusion made to the friend of the family, who furnishes all the children with holiday toys, every one of which has either a crucifying squeak or a stunning explosive power, which soon fits their amiable mother for a lunatic asylum. Nothing is said, as I can find, of that mistress of a family to whom the morning hours are as precious as gold dust, and who is called down to see a gentleman, who (having read *Jones* on the door-plate) straightway, with sublime assurance, asks "for *Mrs*. Jones, on particular business;" when that lady, descending, finds a well-dressed, well-groomed individual, who, with a smirk and a bow, straightway draws from his pocket " a bottle of furniture polish," which he exhausts all the dictionary and her patience in extolling; or presents to her notice a " cement for broken china," or "samples of needles." Scarcely has she rid herself of this nuisance, when " a boy wishes also to see *Mrs. Jones* on particular business," which turns out to be the hoped-for sale of " six envelopes, two steel-pens, a pencil, a brass breast-pin, a tin trumpet, a corkscrew, and four sheets of letter-paper—all for sixpence—*and just sold three next door, mum.*"

Is not the boarding-house public an army of martyrs? As to boarding-house life, I detest it every way: its public feeding, its scandal, its heterogeneousness, its tyrannical edicts against babies and young children, its stifling atmosphere of roast, and boil, and stew, and tobacco-smoke, its punctual delivery of your letters and parcels, *on the entry table ;* its way of sweeping your room at most inconvenient hours, and dusting it with one summary whisk from a long-handled, feather-tailed switch ; its convenient deafness to the jerk of your bell-wire ; its homœopathic coffee and pie ; its towels, threadbare in quality, and niggardly in quantity ; its parlor, showy and shabby, with its inevitable centre-table, with its perennial annuals, its hump-backed rocking-chair, and distorted pictures—and apoplectic bills.

The necessity it entails of always wearing a mask ; of fearing to speak, lest you should tread on the toes of your neighbor's pet hobby, and thereby deprive yourself of the convenient bridge over which the salt and pepper must necessarily travel to your plate, waiters being stupid and scarce; the bore of talking when you feel taciturn, or having your neighbor provokingly insist upon it that you must be ill; the bore of laughing when you feel sad, and hearing threadbare topics rediscussed, and stale jokes resurrectionized; the misery of never being able to have the first unfolding of your own morning-paper, or of having it incontinently disappear, in company with some unprincipled boarder bound on a daybreak journey, and that day sure to be aggravatingly dull and rainy; the necessity of always turning your keys upon boxes and trunks, and the certainty of losing or misplacing them when you are in a double-twisted, insane hurry; your contracted, closetless space; your inevitable city window prospect of back sheds, with ghostly garments hanging on groaning clothes-lines; of distracted bachelors at upper chamber-windows, vainly essaying to sew on missing buttons, and muttering inaudible oaths at their clumsy, needle-pricked fingers.

Now, if you needs must board, go to the biggest and best hotel you can find, where everybody is too much occupied to interfere with your personal business; where waiters are plenty, and it is not high treason to ask for salt with your meat. If your finances forbid this, then, in mercy to yourself, rent a shanty where no third person is a fixture in your family, where you can sneeze when your nose has a call that way, and where your hopes and fears, joys and sorrows will not be leisurely dissected by the cool fingers of malignity, and where that nightmare, Paul Pry-ism, is not always astride of your heart and brain.

That's my opinion of boarding-houses, and may the gods have mercy on the *bored*. Let us have a new edition of Fox at once.

An Error to Avoid.—All writers do best who depict that which they have seen with their own eyes, instead of their "mind's eye." It is very easy to detect the difference. There is a glow, a naturalness, a fidelity to life in the first, that is never to be found in the last. And yet how many, stepping past their own legitimate points of observation, and looking only through the fog of imagination, give us dim, distorted, crude caricatures of life and human beings, the counterpart of which never has and never will exist. This is especially the fault of beginners, whose misdirected aim it is to startle and astonish.

WRITING "COMPOSITIONS."

I HAVE lately received a letter which it would be well every teacher and parent in the land should read. As I shall not betray the name or residence of the distressed young writer, of whom I have no knowledge except what is communicated by her letter, and as it may call attention to the last-drop-in-the-bucket misery, inflicted upon children already sufficiently overtasked, who are required to furnish ideas upon a given subject, which it is utterly impossible their young minds should grasp, I shall make no apology for transcribing it verbatim; calling particular attention to the italicized passages:

"DEAR AUNT FANNY:—You have said you are Auntie to all poor girls in distress. I am in distress, if ever anybody was; and I know that you will be kind to me. Let me tell you about it. I have expected to graduate in about two weeks; and I have no essay to read, and if I don't have one I can't graduate. I would not care so much for that myself, but my father would be *so* disappointed; and he has made so many sacrifices to keep me at school, that I *can't* disappoint him. Oh! I have worked so hard to keep up with my class, for I am obliged to be absent so much, and now if I can't go through, *I shall die, I know.* I am not afraid of passing examination, for I know I can do that successfully, but I never could write any kind of a decent composition; and now it seems as though it was worse than ever, for *I have tried for four months to write one, but I am farther off from it than ever.* I know that you will think me very, *very* dull, and I suppose I am; but, oh! Aunt Fanny, *do, do* pity me. Please, *please* write me one to read—*you* can do it in a very short time. I know that it is a very great favor to ask of you, and I should not dare to do it, but oh! I am almost crazy, and I know by your writings that you will pity and help me. I pray every night that God will help me, and I think He put it into my heart to write to you about it. I have tried everything. Oh, dear! I can't write on anything at all. *I have sat up all night, but I am as dull as ever, and I dream about it when I go to sleep.* Oh! Aunt Fanny, do, *do* pity me, and write for me. I will do anything in this wide world for you. Oh, please, do; I will never forget you. You can do anything almost; I will bless you forever. *Oh, I shall die if I don't have one!* Do write me a line, anyway, and direct to ———, ———. Excuse me for writing so, but I am nearly desperate. *Oh, for the love of God, do write me one in two weeks, or at most three!* I dare not even read over what I have written to you. Oh! Aunt Fanny, don't refuse me."

A better comment than this touching letter, upon the present forcing, hot-house system of education, even I should not desire. Think of this young girl, goaded to the very verge of insanity by those who *should know* that they are defeating the very object they are trying to attain by forcing the young mind to string together to order, and by the page, *words without ideas.* In my opinion this "composition" business is the greatest possible nonsense. I believe it to be the baneful root of the inflated style of writing so prevalent. I believe that there are exercises in English, which would serve the purpose millions of times better without driving pupils mad, and without offering them a premium for deceit, in passing off as their own the thoughts of others. Not long since, I received a letter from the principals of a school, enclosing "a composition" to which "a prize" had just been awarded, and which some person present at the reading had detected as stolen from one of my books; with a request that I would look it over and pronounce upon the same. I found it word for word as I had written it in my book! Perhaps the *moral* effect of this system may be worth inquiring into, even by those who seem to be utterly insensible to the wretched spectacle of a young head tossing feverishly, night after night, on the pillow, under the brooding nightmare of an unwritten "*composition.*" Let careless parents, who are quite as much to blame as teachers, give this subject a thought.

Now, girls, I fully sympathize with you in your

distractions in this dilemma, but this is not the way to help you out of it. I advise you to ask your teacher to allow you to describe some scene or place you have visited, which you could easily do; then write it out naturally, as if you were telling it to some friend, without any attempt at fine language. Also ask your teacher to allow you *to stop when you get through,* instead of exacting so many lines or pages when your ideas give out. That is the only way that good " compositions " can be written, and I wish fervently all school-teachers knew it, and ceased bothering poor young heads " to make bricks without straw," or resort in their distress to the deception you propose to me.

" Composition day," it is true, in my school-days, was only a delight to me. But you should have seen the idiot I was in arithmetic or algebra, or historical dates! How I pinched the girl next me to help me out; and how gratefully I remembered it, in after years, and embroidered my gratitude on her first baby's little flannel petticoats!

Now, my dear young ladies, don't be discouraged because you are slow at " composition." As I say, it is not your fault, for half the time the most impossible subjects are given you to write about. Your minister might just as well be asked to write a dissertation on French millinery. Then, though your gift may not be " composition," it may lie in something quite as important; so with this little consolation I leave you to wriggle out of your dilemma the best way you can, without pilfering.

And, moreover, I think a meeting of school-teachers ought speedily to be called to consider this composition subject and make it, as easily might be done, a delight, instead of a bore and a cheat.

THE LITTLE ONES.—Fortunate are those parents who have learned to respect the *individuality* of their children. Who are not madly bent upon planting them in the family garden in set rows, and so closely that their branches have no room to stretch out into the fair sunlight. Who are not forever on hand with the pruning-knife or hoe, to lop off that which, if left, would develop into sweet buds or flowers; or to dig the earth prematurely from roots which were better left safely hidden till their natural period of vigorous appearing. A gardener who should be guilty of such folly would be a laughing-stock. What if all his flowers were of one color? What if every twig and leaf were of the same size? How weary should we be of this monotony. How we should long for the delicate pink of the rose, and the royal purple of the violet, and the pure snow of the lily, and the distinctive aroma of each! Why not in this respect take a lesson from Nature, which is at once so bountiful and so wise?

NICE LITTLE TEA-PARTIES.

HOSPITALITY seems to be an extinct virtue. Grand parties we have in plenty of all kinds, where those who have vitality sufficient to attend them, and purses long enough to compete with the vulgar show attending them, may return such hollow civilities, and "have it over," as they express it.

"*Have it over!*" There's just the fly in the ointment. The old-fashioned, genuine hospitality never was "over." Nobody wanted it "over." A simple, elegant little tea, a well-cooked, well-served, plain family dinner, one's friend was always welcome to join, without a printed card of invitation weeks beforehand, accompanied with a whispered, "I hope to gracious they won't accept!" But that, alas! is all in the past. Fashion has decreed an elaborate show of food, dishes, and dress. Families pinch themselves a whole year for one grand display of this kind, in the endeavor to compete with those whose means perhaps may justify this barren style of entertaining, and where stupefaction and a consequent lack of intelligent conversation are the only result, save a long bill of expense. The consequence is, that people whose time is valuable, and whose vitality is too precious to expend in this way, refuse all such invitations. But the unfortunate part of it is, that many of them do not revive the old simple hospitality; and when expostulated with upon setting a better example, only reply, that the prevailing taste for show has so vitiated everything, that there are few who care to go where it is not the order of the entertainment.

Now we don't believe this. We have too often heard sensible, cultivated, refined men and women deplore it, to credit this idea. But they are in the mäelstrom; Mrs. So and So is a particular friend, and "she thinks she must go through with this vulgar parade," or, "her husband likes it;" and "they think every time that they accept, they never will do it again, even for her," etc. Now it isn't that there are "few who don't like it:" but it *is* true that there are few who have the independence to inaugurate a different state of things—to be *truly* hospitable without excessive upholstery, or gastronomy, or fine millinery.

To my mind, there is something better than sitting hours to see servants dexterously place and take away dishes. One sees that at home in lesser degree, and with less waste of time. One can converse with one's hostess there, and she will not answer at random, because her mind is occupied with processions of birds and sugar and wines. Little children's faces, like flowers, are there, in place of a stiff bouquet of flowers and silver pyramids obscuring one's *vis-à-vis*. *There* is a home flavor which puts the most modest guest at ease, and permits him or her to bring forth something in the way of conversation that is not the inflamed product of half a dozen kinds of wine—something to remember and think of afterward with pleasure, instead of blushing next day to associate with the speaker.

I say there are people, and the best kind of people too, who *much* prefer this style of entertainment; but they should not rest there. They should inaugurate something better in their place, instead only of retiring in disgust under the shelter of their own roofs, and living only for their own family circles. They owe a duty also to society, and it should be paid by setting a sensible example of old-fashioned simplicity in hospitality, which in time may reform this matter. People who value their brains want them in decent condition for the next morning, and the next morning after that, and cannot afford to waste them in this manner. It is a matter of dollars and cents with them, I'd have you to know, as well as a matter of taste ; if, indeed, I may be pardoned for putting forward an idea so practical. They wish to retire early, for one thing; they prefer outdoor air for another, when they are off duty with the pen, instead that of a close, stifled room, and the spectacle of feeding and drinking till sense and wit give out. This is plain talking, but it won't hurt you, my friends, to have a little occasionally.

A SLEEPLESS NIGHT.

YOU know what it is to lie awake at night, I suppose, while every lumpish human creature in the house is sleeping, regardless of the perspiration standing in drops on your bewitched forehead; regardless of your twitching fingers, and kicking toes, and glaring, distended eyes; regardless of your increasing disgust at each miserable moment at the monotonous tap, tap, tap, of solitary heels on the forsaken sidewalk; regardless of your meditated vengeance on the morrow, should you perchance survive to see it, upon the owner of that flapping-blind across the way, which has been slamming fore-and-aft all night, and yet never dropped, as you hoped it might, on somebody's or anybody's head—you didn't care whose, so that you might have been delivered from the nuisance.

In vain have you tried the humbugging recipe of saying the Multiplication Table; in vain have you repeated poetry by the yard, or counted one hundred; in vain have you conjugated verbs, or done any of the foolish things recommended in such cases. *Two* o'clock has just struck, and no somniferous result has followed. Well—if you can't sleep, you *won't* sleep, that's all. You'll just get up, and strike a light and read. You do it; but the fire is low, and cold shivers run up and down your back-bone You're hungry! yes—that must be it. You'll go to the closet, and get a bit of cold chicken you wot of. Good heavens! if those lumpish, snoring wretches haven't devoured it before going to bed. You go look at the creature vindictively; *you* know just who would be capable of such a meanness. She has slept there these three hours, on the strength of that bit of purloined chicken—*your* chicken—while you haven't closed an eyelash. She *will* sleep comfortably till daylight; and get up with a clear head, and refreshed limbs, to breakfast. Then she will eat, like a great healthy animal, while food looks perfectly nauseous to you, who will then be too exhausted to be hungry. You look at the creature again, and think of Judith and Holofernes; and don't wonder as you used at Judith. Indeed, she seems to you at that moment rather an estimable person than otherwise; and as to pitying Holofernes, why should *you* pity anybody who could *sleep?*

You walk to the window. It is some comfort that the stars have to wink all night as well as you. And there's a policeman, dragging up and down in the cold, and clapping his hands across his breast to keep warm. Good! you're glad of it. Four o'clock! Gracious! how you *will* feel to-morrow. If you only had a bottle of ale to make you stupid and drowsy. And sure enough, now you think of it, there is just one left. You seize it! Why—somebody has unwired the cork. Merciful man! it is only *Ink*. Now, that's a little too much for a tired soul. Suppose you should begin and run from the top of the stairs to the bottom, as fast and as loud as you could, and wake up the whole family. And as the vision of terrified night-gowns rises before your mental vision, you commence grinning noiselessly like a maniac; then laughing hysterically; then crying outright; and the next thing you know it is eight o'clock in the morning, and coffee and rolls and beefsteak are awaiting your advent.

And as to musquitoes. Ah! you too have suffered. You have lain, hour after hour, listening to that never-ceasing war-song, till you were as nervous as a hump-backed cat face to face with Jowler in a corner. You have " turned over; " you have lain on your side, lain on your back, lain on your face, spite of your prominent nose. You have doubled your fists up under your arm-pits, and twisted your feet into hard knots under your night-clothes, to no avail. You have then fallen back on your dignity and the pigmy-ness of your tormentors, and folding your arms resolutely over your chest, and looking fiercely up to the ceiling, exclaimed:

> "Come one—come all—this bed shall fly
> From its stout legs as soon as I!"

And yet, at that very moment, an " owdacious " bite has sent you, with a smothered exclamation, into the middle of the floor, bewailing the day you were born.

Next day you get a " musquito net." What a

fool not to think of it before. You festoon it round your bed. It looks pink-y and safe. You explore it carefully that night before getting in, that no treacherous crevice be left for the enemy. You put out the light, and oh! happiness unutterable, listen to their howl of rage *outside*, which sounds like the "music of the spheres," and fall asleep. Next morning you wake with a splitting headache. Can it be the confined air of the net? *Horrible!* You spend that day nursing your head and your wrath. Why were musquitoes made? You find no satisfactory solution. What do they live on when not devouring human beings? Why, in the same bed, is one bitten and the other left? Why infest New York, and leave Brooklyn, whose inhabitants deserve punishment for monopolizing Beecher? Why, if they *must* bite, not pitch in at once, instead of stopping to harrow you by giving a concert.

That night you refuse to gasp under a net, for all the musquitoes that ever swarmed. You even light your gas defiantly, open the windows, and sneer at the black demons as they buzz in for their nocturnal raid. You sit and read—occasionally boxing your own ears—till the small hours, and then—to bed; only to dash frantically against the wall, throw your pillows at the enemy, laugh hysterically, and rise at daylight a blear-eyed, spotted, dismal wretch!

WOMEN'S NEED OF RECREATION.

I READ an article the other day on working-men's clubs, which set me thinking. In it was set forth the necessity, after a man's hard day's work, of an evening of rest, away from home, where he should find light and warmth, and boon companionship, other than is to be found in the corner grocery.

Now this is well, were there not a better way, as I believe. I am not about to propose clubs for working-women, because our police reports show every day that they have existed for a long time—thanks to "corner groceries"—and that they are made of any implement that comes handy, and result in bruised flesh and a broken head. This being the case, I cannot see why the working-woman, as well as the working-man, does not need, after a hard day's work, "light, warmth, and boon companionship of an evening, away from home." Nay, all the more, since work, hard as her husband may, it is often in the fresh, open air; or, if not, he has it going and returning, and the boon companionship of his fellow-workmen with it; while she, with "Ginx's last baby" to look after, in some noisome tenement house, stands over the perpetual wash-tub or cooking-stove, with two or three half-grown children hanging to her draggled skirts, never exchanging her unwomanly rags, not even perhaps to mass for a hurried prayer in the church which, God be thanked, is free alike to poor and rich, and which suggests, in its own way, a distant heaven for her.

Thinking over all this, I said why not Germanize this thing? Why not have clubs for working-men and their families, with innocent amusement minus the drink? Isn't it possible? Or if not, I wish it were, for the poor harassed women's sake. I only see the millennial germ of it; but this I know, that the wives need it more, far more, than their husbands, the wide world over, and in every strata of society; by the pains of motherhood, even in favorable conditions; by her intenser nervous organization; by her indoor confinement and narrowing, petty detail-worries; by the work that ends not at sundown as does his. By the wakeful, unrestful nights, which every mother knows; *this* is the hardest, most wearing kind of work, no matter what may be said of the husband, who has his sleep at least; who demands *that* in every family exigency as his right, and as the foundation of his ability to labor for his family. Ah! what if the wife and mother, with less strength, feebler organization, should make a stand for this? even when, in addition to her other cares, she helps in some outside honest way to support the family?

Does she not, too, need warmth, light, and boon

companionship of an evening? While it is true that
> "All work and no play
> Makes Jack a dull boy,"

remember it is just as true of Jack's wife as it is of Jack, and the founders of "Working-men's Clubs" would do well to put this into their foundation.

I wish that some of the pains taken to make human beings "*good*" were expended in trying to make them *happy*. Particularly is this necessary in regard to young people, though it is a fact that should be recognized much more than it is, in the conditions of every human being. Let a little sunshine into the outward circumstances surrounding them before you begin to talk about a future state. There are children, and grown people too, so cobwebbed over with care and misery, that all talk, how "*good*" soever, is useless. *They want some brightness infused into their lives.* It may be a wife—weary, body and soul; tired of plodding; she needs some kind voice to say (alas! how little husbands think of it!): "Come, leave all your cares just *now, this minute*, and if you can't leave without I take your place, I'll take it, and it will be a gain to both of us; for you have come just to that spot where you must stop to rest, or fail entirely." It may be a little child under your care, perhaps your own, perhaps another's; who is not really "*bad*," but only troublesome. It wants change; a ramble in the Park, or a ramble somewhere; something to see and talk about, and *happify* it; some new objects to occupy its mind and thoughts; and the more intelligent the child is, the more necessary this becomes. Many a child is punished because its active mind, having no food, becomes a torment to itself and others. *Give it food!* Take it up to the Park and show it the animals there. Tell it of their habits, and the way they live in the countries from which they were taken. This is a *cheap* pleasure, it is true, and may, though it ought not to be, a very commonplace one to you; but you have no idea how it freshens the mind and body of the little one. *Sometimes I almost think that happiness is goodness.* Certainly, till the hard and difficult lesson of life is thoroughly learned, it is wise to lend a helping hand to those who are stumbling after, lest they fall by the way to rise no more.

Perhaps you have some good servants in your house whose underground, plodding life needs relief, who have grown sharp and querulous on account of it; whose lot needs brightening a bit. Send them or take them to some place of amusement; give them a holiday, or half a holiday if you can do no better. You have no idea how this break in their wearisome round will lighten toil for many a day; and more because *you thought of it*, perhaps, than from the pleasure the amusement afforded.

Life presses heavily on most of us in one shape or another. They are not always the greatest sufferers, whose barrel of meal and cruse of oil fail. Therefore, when I open a church door, and the first sentence I hear is about " An *Awful* God," I sometimes want to invite the speaker to rest himself a bit, and let me try my hand at it. I believe that most people want soothing, and comforting, and encouraging, more than denouncing or frightening, even though the latter be done with good intentions. I know most *women* have been " punished " enough during the week, without being threatened with it in another world on Sundays. Take that poor soul with a drunken husband, who tries to support him and herself, and no end of children, by washing, and whose husband comes home only to demand her money, and smash up her wash-tub and table and chairs for his amusement. Would you talk to that woman about an " *awful God*," when she stole away to church for a crumb of comfort on Sunday ? You had much better buy her a new wash-tub, and put her brute of a husband where—but it won't do to say all one thinks, even out of " meetin'."

THE GOOD OLD HYMNS.

DID you never know any person who was brought up on the good old *Zion-hymns*, whom they ever failed to move to the foundations when heard? The feet moving on unholy errands linger on their way past the church door, as the melody floats out upon the air. That man—who has wasted life, and energy, and talent, which might have blessed mankind, to reap only the whirlwind—he is back again with his little head upon his mother's lap, while she sings that same hymn, which will never grow old, about "the beautiful river." His eyes moisten as he thinks how pained she would be, were she living, to know him now. The hymn ceases, and the low benediction follows, and as the worshippers emerge, he recollects himself, and with an impatient pshaw! passes on. What, *he* moved at a "conventicle hymn"? *He*, who for years has never crossed the threshold of a church! He? who believes neither in prayer nor priests, Bible nor Sundays? He, who has "outgrown all that"? Ah! but he hasn't. He *can't* outgrow it. It is *there*. It *will* come, whether he desires it or no. Come in spite of all his efforts to laugh or reason it away. Come, though he lives in open derision and mockery of that religion whose divine precepts he cannot efface from his mind. Come, as it did to John Randolph, who, after years of atheism and worldliness and ambition, left on record, "that the only men he ever knew well and approached closely, whom he did not discover to be unhappy, were sincere believers of the Gospel, who conformed their lives, as far as the nature of man can permit, to its precepts." "Often," he says, "the religious teachings of his childhood were banished wholly by business or pleasure; but after a while they came more frequently, and stayed longer, until at last they were his first thoughts on waking and his last before going to sleep." Said he, "I could not banish them if I would."

"Now and then I like to go into a church," said a young man apologetically to a companion who was deriding the idea. "Priestcraft! priestcraft!" exclaimed his companion. "Tell me what possible good can it do you?" "Well," said the young man, "somehow, when I hear those hymns it is like hearing the pleading voice of my mother as I left home to become the graceless fellow I am now. I cannot tell you how they move me, or how they make me wish I were better. If I ever do become better, it will be because I cannot separate them from all that seems, in my better moments, worth embodying in the word 'home.'" Walter Scott said to his son-in-law, when he was on his death-bed, "Be a *good* man, Lockhart—be a good man; nothing else will give you any comfort when you come to lie here." It were easy to multiply instances where earth's gifted and greatest have borne similar testimony, after having tested all that the world had to offer, as an equivalent for "that peace which passeth all understanding."

Parents sometimes say with tears, my boy has forgotten all my teachings. You don't *know* that. You can't *say* that till the grave closes over him. Said a good mother I knew, who kept on singing those hymns, and whose faith never faltered through long years, when her only son disgraced the family by intemperance, "John will come right by and by. He *must*." And day after day, when he was brought home helpless, the mere wreck and libel of manhood, she smilingly repeated to all cavillers: "John will come right. I *know* it. Every day I ask God to *give him back to himself*, and I *know* He will do it."

And John *did* come right. Out of that horrible pit of degradation he emerged "clothed and in his right mind." He is now in good business standing, owns the house he lives in, is the comfort and pride of the patient wife who, with his mother, waited woman-like, *Christ-like*, all those weary years for his return. I myself have seen him in church, when the Sacramental wine was passed to him, bow his head reverently and humbly over the cup without raising it to his lips.

Never despair of a child who strays away from *those hymns*. Somewhere between the cradle and the tomb be sure those hymns will find him out.

Only he to whom heaven is a reality, can possibly

preserve his self poise in the jarring conflict of life. How can man, constantly disheartened and disappointed as he is, by the *apparent* triumph of wrong over right, by the poverty of those of whom the world is not worthy, in contrast with the gilded, full-fed, honored wickedness which seems to give the lie to everything to which our better natures cling, how can man, under such circumstances, walk hopefully in the narrow path, if beyond and through the mists of the valley he discerns not the serene mountain-tops? No—only the Christian can say in view of earthly loss and disappointments: "It is well—let *Him* do what seemeth to Him good." Only the Christian—nor need he be—nor is he—*of necessity* a "church member,"—can say—"Though He slay me, yet will I trust in Him."

LADIES, DON'T DO IT.—Every modest woman should set her face against any fashion which could for a moment identify her with those women who have no claim to modesty, no matter how "stylish" that fashion may be termed. This word "stylish" has much to answer for in this regard. Dr. Johnson's rule was a good one: "Dress so that no person can possibly remember what you have on." Unfortunately, the reverse of this rule is that which is generally aimed at, even by women who in other matters command respect.

A STRANGER IN GOTHAM.

THIS unfortunate is easily recognized in New York, by its frantic bewilderment in attempting to cross Broadway; now standing still, now leaping forward, now running back, in that agony of indecision which is the best and surest recipe for a broken neck. Also by walking with its mates three abreast, in that crowded thoroughfare, as if room was as plenty there as in its native Frogtown. Another sure sign of its origin is in its continuous and demonstrative waving of the handkerchief, umbrella, parasol, basket, or any other weapon handy, at a desired omnibus driver, who of course knows a native at once by the quiet uplifted forefinger. Once inside the omnibus, the stranger may be known, by ferreting anxiously in all his pockets for a five-dollar bill, instead of handing up the ready sixpence with which the native avoids eternal self-reproach and the maledictions of hurried fellow-passengers. Also, the stranger may be known by his extreme and stunning toggery at places of public amusement, where fashion chooses to sit in quiet raiment.

If the stranger is a Bostonian, he may at once be recognized by wearing—without regard to his profession—a sepulchral suit of solemn black, with immaculately polished boots and bosom, and a stand-aside-I-am-holier-than-thou air, intended to crush the sons of Belial who behold it. Let it not be supposed, however, by the uninitiated, that this, by any means, precludes him from joining any gay or festive scene which New York holds out as a reward of merit, to any inflated Pharisee, for a prolonged and painful spell of good behavior.

The stranger within the gate is sometimes the angel unawares; in which case she may be seen innocently and promiscuously distributing pennies, here and there, among bogus "objects of charity," and feeling good, as she takes a last pitiful look at the painted ulcer on the l—imb as sound as her own. Or she may be seen, verdantly buying one of those huge cabbage bouquets, in alternate mutton-chop streaks of white and red, got up for the delectation of strangers, and pensively applying it to her gratified nose, when her head is not spinning a teetotum after some new freak of fashion, as displayed in a new arrangement of passing feather, ribbon, or bow.

As if the equilibrium of a New Yorker could be disturbed by any such trifles! No. Omnibus horses may rise and fall, like the waves of the sea. "Extra" boys may yell themselves black in the face. Regiments in all the hues of the *reign-beau*, may come and go; but unless somebody knocks the well-beloved cigar from his jaded lip, Satan may claim him for his own, for aught he would move a muscle.

MY JOURNEY TO QUEBEC AND BACK AGAIN.

IF there is a feeling akin to Heaven, it is to reach home after a long journey. And this I take to be quite consistent with great enjoyment of all the beautiful things and places one has seen in one's absence—aye, and people, too. To sit down in your own dear old chair, and kick your slippers across the room; to talk without being overheard; to eat with only those whom you love about you—for this promiscuous hotel-feeding is repulsive to me beyond the power of expression. I think I am peculiar on this point, but it seems to me as great an individual profanation as to admit the same number of people to see you perform your toilette for dinner. That there are people to whom it is one of the delights of travel to sit down to such hecatombs of food with such a menagerie of human beings, I am well aware. I am not one of them.

The first place we visited was Saratoga; don't be frightened. I leave "New York correspondents" of newspapers all over the country to give fabulous accounts of fabulous belles, and the number of their lovers, which will very generally be found to correspond with the number of their trunks. I am not going to venture on so hackneyed a theme, hotel life being the same at Saratoga as anywhere else—simply one eternal dress and eat. The *place itself* was what I went to see—the springs—the grounds—not the peacocks that were in them. The ornamental grounds attached to the springs are very lovely and attractive, as well as faultlessly kept, affording abundant opportunities to sighing lovers and bread-and-butter maidens. Contrary to my expectations, I found the waters very palatable, though, were I compelled by fashion to wash down my morning orisons with ten or twelve tumblers full, I might change my mind. It is curious how long they have bubbled up there, as freely as now, the Indians having partaken of them a fabulous time back. The fountain might be made more attractive, did some pretty girl do the tumbler-dipping for visitors, instead of the matter-of-fact jacket and trousers who handed it to us—I merely throw this in as a suggestion. We stepped into a shop opposite the springs, to see the operation of bottling and corking the waters performed by machinery; the celerity with which this was accomplished was very gratifying to my Yankee chain-lightning notion of things, and being a Yankee, of course it was not out of my line to think what a very nice piece of property it must be to hold, for this and other palpable reasons. I trust all the sentimental Misses who have had "offers" over those tumblers of water will forgive me.

Stepping into one or two shops in the village, to hunt up some nick-nacks for a dear little girl at home, I encountered some familiar New York shop faces. One woman told me that she hired a shop there every year during the "season," and that many other New-Yorkers did the same, retreating again when the tide of fashion set cityward. They calculate rightly—the shopping mania never will be burned out of women while there is a timber left of her; and were there nothing but an old horse-blanket in the village, she would buy it, if she had to throw it away the next minute. I wish it to be understood that I do not share this furore of my sex, as I never enter a shop of my own free will, until my clothes show signs of dropping off my back unless replaced.

The lady visitors at Saratoga get themselves up most stunningly, to walk through the streets to the springs, with their white embroidered petticoats peeping from beneath their rainbow-colored silk morning-dresses, and black-lace veils thrown Spanish fashion over their heads, making unhandsome faces, if only refined, look picturesque. This annual wave of folly, said I, must send its ripples farther than the circumference of this village. I had hardly made the remark, before two barrel-shaped country lasses passed, with tawdry, cheap imitations in délaine of the Saratoga silk morning-dress, and with coarse black veils thrown round their sunburnt faces. It was a capital burlesque, though, I assure you, the maidens themselves were far from regarding it in that light.

The private cottages on the grounds of the hotel,

for families and parties who choose to live by themselves, are nice little cosey affairs. This is a much pleasanter, and, to my mind, a much more civilized arrangement than living at the public hotel; but, as the execrable organ-grinder wouldn't stop playing for sixpence, so the landlord, knowing well the value of peace and quietness, charges accordingly.

From Saratoga we went the usual route to Lake George, performing the last miles by stage coach. That's nice, thought I,—a change of conveyance wonderfully eases the limbs—*i. e.*, if they are not past easing. I was hasty;—a heavy rain set in, and came driving first into the windows, through which, at the risk of dislocating our elbows, we spread our umbrellas for spouts. Then the roof began to leak, and gentlemen shrugged the shoulders of their linen travelling coats, and whispered, "Rheumatism;" and ladies benevolently offered the corners of their travelling cloaks and shawls to the victims; and temporary plugs were made for the roof, of "The New York Times," which we found "would not hold water;" and night came on, and the rain grew more persistent, and we got accustomed to sitting in a puddle; and the wheels sank in the mud, and the old coach "tetered"—as the children say—now this side, now that, and the most inveterate joker of the party had long been dumb; when the coachman, who had been jogging on in a helpless, despairing way, gave his whip the professional crack, which sent our noses up to the roof for a last final rub, and the wet, draggled, muddy, hungry, dead-and-alive crew were dragged out piecemeal over the wheels of the coach, on to the piazza of the "Fort William Henry Hotel," where were a swarm of colored waiters, where was a band of music on the piazza, where was a sumptuous parlor of interminable length—mirror, tête-à-tête, and piano. But, unfortunately, none of all those could we eat or drink. Woman wants but little here below, but I'll tell all you landlords what she does want. After sitting in a puddle, beside enduring a shower-bath at the same time through the roof of the coach, a *hot* cup of tea it *might* not be unreasonable for her to expect. It is very well for men to "pooh!"—they can afford to be philosophical—they who run to the bar-room and get "set up," as they call it, on their arrival, or console themselves for cold tea, sour berries, and tough beefsteak, with the infallible cigar.

The question is how their philosophy would hold out if there were *no* cigars to be had, and *no* bar-room, and they were shaking in an ague of cold? I hate a fussy woman who is always digging down to the bottom of hotel salt-cellars, and microscopically inspecting potatoes; but I will say, that when every thread of a woman's raiment is dripping, it takes a more angelic being than I am to go shivering to bed on a cup of cold tea, past an army of darkies whom you are too vexed with their employer to bribe.

The next morning it still rained, and as there was no inducement in-doors to remain, our breakfast being worse than our tea of the night before, we made our escape into the little steamer "Minnehaha" to see Lake George; and lovely it was, spite of fog, and mist, and rain, as we glided away between its green shores, and past its fairy islands, startling out the little birds from their leafy nests into short, swift circles over our heads, then back again, where never perhaps, since the creation, man's foot has trod.

Lake George is a little gem, though we saw it only through a vale of mist, the sun absolutely refusing to brighten it up for one brief moment. "Such a pity. It must be surpassingly lovely on a fine day," we all kept saying to one another, as we anxiously watched the gray clouds. Everybody seemed to be in good spirits, however, and some ladies, more romantic than wise, took their stations on the upper deck, spite of the slanting rain and mist, giving their gentlemen friends constant employment in tucking shawls round their feet and shoulders, till they looked like bandaged mummies. After a while they came down, and I saw certain mysterious-looking flasks drawn from the aforementioned gentlemen's pockets, and held to their blue lips, by which token I concluded that brandy sometimes does for a woman what sentiment will not.

And now again the old lumbering stage-coach is in requisition for a seven-mile jog, and trot, and plough through the mud, and we pack in, like layers of herring, and there is plenty of joking and laughing, for many of the party are young and merry, and it was blessed to listen to their ringing laughter, and look upon their bright eyes. Many a good thing was said, though had it not been half as good, we were all prepared to laugh upon the slightest provocation, for our legs and arms were bundled up in such a way, as rendered "dignity" quite out of the question, and gravity an impossibility. At last we arrived (I declare I believe they called the thing a "hotel") at the foot of Lake Champlain, where we were to dine. "Be advised by me," said one of the lady passengers to me, "and don't go in to dinner. I did it once, and since, when I stop here, I bring my own sandwiches." It is sometimes fun to sit down to a two-pronged-fork dinner, and the rest of us were in the humor for whatsoever the gods sent, so in we went. The staple commodities of the table were soft huckleberries and fried fish. Two girls—daughters, I suppose, of our host—waited upon table; that is to say, they rotated in a certain ghostly fashion, with their arms hanging by their sides, and their eyes fixed upon the floor, and were about as much use as two statues on castors, as it was impossible to catch either their eyes or attention. "What on earth is a fellow to call them?" asked one hungry man. "Waiter!"—that didn't appeal to them. "Girl!" it was no use. "You, there!" in a tone of impatience. The rock of Gibraltar couldn't have stood it better.

Now, if this was a preconcerted bashfulness, it worked admirably, for we could get nothing that was not immediately before us, unless some philanthropic fellow-sufferer, in pity, sent a pie spinning à la Ravel, down the table. Well, at any rate we had our money's worth of fun, and could bear it much better than if the parlor had been resplendent with mirrors, sofas, tête-à-têtes, and "grand pianos," which so often pave the way for a terrible disappointment as to everything else. We expected little, and got less; but those imperturbable, ghostly girls cost me, many a time and oft during the rest of my journey, a button or a hook and eye, as the picture came up before me.

Talk of Lake George. It is to Lake Champlain what a pretty, little, simpering, pink-and-white doll of a girl is to a magnificent woman, the royal sweep of whose robe about her faultless limbs as she moves, sets all the pulses wild. In mercy to us the clouds parted, and the bright sun broke through at last. You should have seen it then—the queenly Lake Champlain—with the bold, dark islands that seemed to float upon its silvery smoothness, with the heavy rain-clouds gathering up their forces, and gliding majestically away in the distance, leaving a sky as soft and blue as ever arched over Eden. On one side the broad, green, cultivated fields, stretched away fair in the sunlight; on the other, pile upon pile, were the huge, dark mountains, up whose steep sides the soft mist was wreathing itself in a thousand fantastic, graceful shapes. It was a moment such as all of us have sometimes known, when pleasure is so intense as to become almost pain; when language fails; when the eye fills, and there seems more "Bible" between the blue covers of sea and sky than you ever looked upon, or listened to, before, and everywhere you turned, a voice—"the still small voice"—seemed saying, all this I made for *you*—for *you*. Now you might thunder the "terrors of the law" in my ears ten months, and it would not move me; but I feel like the veriest wretch alive, when I so intensely enjoy that for which my daily life is so paltry a return.

The boat in which we performed this trip was a Yankee boat, called "The America," and it was enough to rouse one's patriotism to go through it; the shining neatness of its decks and cabins; its efficient and well-mannered stewardess, always on hand, yet never in the way, understanding, as if by intuition, what everybody wanted; the nice, hot, orderly supper, with waiters that had ears, and knew how to use their feet. I was glad it was named "The America." I was as proud of the beautiful boat as if I had laid her keel. But all pleasures must have an end; and our destination being Montreal, we were soon to leave thrifty, go-ahead Yankee-land and all its peculiarities behind. As we passed the pretty town of Burlington, the residence of the poet "Saxe," we all waved him our most cordial good wishes, which we trust the winds bore him safely.

Upon leaving the boat for the cars, which were to take us to Montreal—Imprimis, a hideous, cavernous looking depot, with one poor, miserable lamp to help us break our necks by—a great talk of "custom-house officers examining trunks," and "smuggling," etc. What a jabbering of French when we took our seat in the cars! and what exorbitant fares for travelling through such a gloomy, God-forsaken, pine-stump, log-cabin looking country! Sleep came to my relief on a safe shoulder, after I had relieved myself by the above speech. At last we reached the funny, foreign, forlorn, cushionless ferry-boat that was to land us in Montreal, and as true as preaching, in got that woman with the *seven babies*, who had traveled with us all day, calm as an oyster in its shell, though the whole seven were screeching alternately and eternally, poor little toads, and still *continued* screeching, with some real or imaginary pain under their aprons. I did hope the poor things were going to bed somewhere; but no, there they sat, bolt upright in the ferry-boat, all in a row—those miserable seven—with their mouths wide open, sending forth the discordant-est cries, and that prolific female never even perspired! but sat with her fat hands folded over her belt, calmly accepting her conjugal destiny! And this is Montreal, said I, as they stood me up on the pier with the trunks, and half deafened with the French jabber about me, I essayed to climb up into a thing (a cross between a New York omnibus and a "Black Maria") that was waiting to convey us to the hotel. And this is Montreal. Well, I shouldn't care if it was Sodom and Gomorrah, if there's only a bed in it. When I mention that our destination was "The Donegana House," every traveller will understand that to be but another name for sumptuous fare and the most assiduous attention at the hands of the handsome landlord and his well-disciplined corps of servants.

In all honesty, I cannot say that I like Montreal. It may be a very substantially built town—I believe that is what they say of it—but one likes beauty as well as strength, and my eye ached for something ornamental in the way of flower-gardens, or, in fact, in any other way. Red coats there were in plenty, but they did not supply the deficiency. Then the never-ceasing bell-ringing, from early dawn to sunset, would soon drive me as mad as our "glorious Fourth," does every year, when gunpowder and bells and cannon have it all their own way, till one is tempted to wish one never had any "forefathers."

Of course the first thing that we saw at Montreal, as also at Quebec, was "*New York Ledger Out*," all over the Canadian walls; and nobody can compute the thousands they said were sold there, so that I may get a boxed ear for saying what I have about Montreal, and as there is a possibility of it, I might as well be cuffed for half a dozen things as one, and so I'll go on and free my mind. And to begin with, I confess that I never could understand that curious piece of female mechanism, an English woman, who is shocked almost into fits at the way American women move, act, and have their independent being generally; who can get along with nothing but yea and nay, thee and thou, and the most formal, walk-on-a-crack strait-lacedness of demeanor and speech, and iced at that; who is ready to hold up hands of holy horror at the idea of an American parent or guardian allowing a young girl to be left *alone* with her lover one second before marriage; and yet these pattern icicles will strip (I know it is a shocking word, but it is the only one that will express my meaning), upon going to a ball, or the theatre, with a freedom that would make any decent American woman crimson with shame. I have seen this again and again, and yet the prudes lecture American women upon the proprieties. Truly, great is English propriety! I saw the same English latitude in dress at the theatre in Montreal, where were assembled, with other ladies, many of the wives, daughters, and sweethearts of the English officers. Of course, in a New York theatre the awful voice of fashion would vote a ball-room dress "vulgar;" and even at the opera, where fashion goes to yawn, and whisper, and ogle, ladies, as a general thing, wear their bonnets and opera cloaks, but the fair Montrealites, having but few places of public amusement, made the most of this, and of their personal charms also, and the result was stunning, even to the eye of that model of impropriety, an American woman. Mesdames, let us have no more lectures from English lips on "American female improprieties," till you pick this big beam out of your own eyes. As to the English officers, they were magnificent specimens of manhood; tall, broad-chested, straight-limbed, healthy, muscular, lovable looking men, not at all dependent for their attractiveness either upon epaulette or uniform, with fine bass voices, and a jolly laugh that was a regular heart-warmer to hear.

Of course we saw *the* magnificent cathedral in Montreal. I did not think it necessary, as did a fellow-traveller, one Sir Statistic, who forever had some unhappy wretch by the button, asking about "feet" and "inches," with pencil, paper, and "guide-book" —how I hate a guide-book! I did not think it necessary to inquire how many square feet there were in this immense building; I knew that there was one pair of feet in it that were *not* square, and that had to support the body to which they belonged till they ached for want of a seat, as heretic feet should, I suppose, from a Montreal point of view, though the *locked* empty pews were very tantalizing. The sermon was in French, and if the eye of my old teacher should fall on this, I beg to say to her ladyship, that notwithstanding "she never could tell how *that* girl was ever going to learn French," and notwithstanding "that girl" has never rubbed up said French since she left school, yet she was able to understand the sermon, as also the French signs and labels so abundant in Montreal, as also some French remarks about herself, all the while looking as stupid as she very well knows "that girl" can. But to return to the cathedral. I hold up both hands for the largest liberty of conscience for everybody, and though I could not understand why one set of priests took such tender care of the hind lappets of another set of priests, spreading them reverently over the backs of their chairs for them, whenever they sat down, or why candles were burned in broad daylight, or why some kept sitting, and others kept kneeling, and bowing, and crossing themselves, or why some glided perpetually in and out from behind the altar, or why some swung incense, or why some were dressed in red and white, and some in black, and some in black and white, yet I was glad that this was a country where everybody could worship the way it best pleased him, and I have seen quite too much to condemn in other sects and faiths, to wish to interfere with this. The "confession boxes," some for English sins, some for French sins, some for Spanish sins, labelled each with the name of the human "father" into whose ears they were to be poured, gave me a long fit of thinking. My sins are many, but it is not *there* I would unburden my soul. Still, let all these religious problems work themselves out. For the priests, I must say, in all candor, that I have never seen a body of men—and I scanned them closely whenever and wherever I met them—with more purity, serenity, and perfect good-humored content expressed in their faces. Their life being active and out of doors, may in part explain this; but alas for the nuns! immured in those tomb-like walls; their cheerfullest employment listening to the moans of the sick and the groans of the dying, in the hospital wards under their roofs. I saw them come into chapel two and two, with downcast eyes, and pallid faces, shrouded by the black hood of renunciation, and kneeling on the floor chant their prayers. Oh, the unnaturalness of such seclusion for a woman! If they could but leave outside the walls, upon entering, their human feelings, and really *be* the cold statues they *look;* but God help them, they do not; they are but women still, and some of them young, and one look into their faces told the story. Nothing could exceed the neatness of the nunnery we visited, or the apartments and bedding in them for the sick and disabled. One man whom we saw there had been strapped into his chair like an infant for *twenty-five* years, and there he sat, with a rosary between his helpless fingers, scarcely living, and yet, perhaps, with many a year of patient waiting for release before him. The outer door of the convent was opened for us by a young novice, whose sweet face, framed in pure white muslin bands, was beautiful to see. Poor child, sighed I, and in another moment I thought of the gay, bedizened misery in Broadway, and I said to myself, as I lingered to take another look at her, perhaps 'tis better so, and left her with a lighter heart.

I should not do justice to Montreal were I to omit to mention *the* drive of the place, " round the mountain." A New York gentleman whom we met in Montreal took us round, and I was glad I saw the city at parting to such good advantage; distance brightened it up wonderfully, and the St. Lawrence sparkled as gayly and as innocently in the sunlight, as if its waters did not play the mischief with every traveller who tasted them. There are many fine country-seats round the mountain. We saw, too, a "haunted house" in this ride, and verily, the occupant was a ghost of taste, and had selected for himself most comfortable quarters, commanding as lovely a view as you or I or any other ghost would ever wish to see. I proposed leaving my card for him, with a view to better acquaintance, but the rest of the party were in flesh-and-blood humor, and evidently preferred returning to the manifold creature comforts to be had of our host of the Donegana House. We left next morning for Quebec, of which more anon. My kingdom for a horse-blanket on that misty morning over the ferry! Instead we had two priests, buttoned up to their heels in long black robes, which I wanted most furiously to borrow, for I was shaking with cold, and New York cold and Montreal and Quebec cold, let me tell you, are two quite different things. When you get such a cough fastened on your lungs there as I did, you may believe it.

I liked Quebec much better than Montreal. Of its splendid site it is unnecessary to speak, everybody having either seen it or read of it, and yet how tame seem all descriptions, when, standing upon the ramparts, one tries to take in at a glance the splendid panorama before him. Every inch of ground is historical, and imagination runs riot as you look at the spot where the gallant Burr bore off from the enemy the dead body of the brave Montgomery, or gaze at the monuments erected to Wolfe and Montcalm. The sentinels, pacing up and down with their measured tread, aid in keeping up the illusion; and as the wind whistles past, you start involuntarily, as if expecting a shower of bullets past your ears. And speaking of bullets, the little urchins who lie perdu on the battle-field, watching for unwary travellers, have an inexhaustible stock of them, which they assure you, with precociously grave faces, funny to see, were "*actually* found there," with their wan, dirty little paws; also they exhibit some shining little pebbles, baptized by them "diamonds," all of which we of course pocketed, and paid for, as if there were no humbug in the little speculators; bigger boys than they have told worse fibs in the same line of business—poor little Barnums!

The most unimaginative person could easily fancy himself in a foreign country in Quebec. The motley population—the long, black-robed priests, serving as a foil to the scarlet coats of the officers, and the white uniform worn by the band; the loose-trousered, rolling sailors; the Frenchy, peasant-looking country people, driving into market with their produce in the most ancient of lumbering-looking vehicles, with bright red raspberries, in shining little birch-bark baskets. The healthy-looking female Quebec-ites, with their fanciful dark straw hats, with a fall of black lace about their rosy faces, wonderfully enhancing the brightness of bright eyes, and making even dull ones, if any such there are, look coquettish under this pretty head-dress, so much more comfortable than our little minikin bonnets, and worn alike by mothers and daughters. Their dresses almost even with their ankles, and little or no crinoline, but such healthy, rosy faces, such luxuriant locks, and the universal little band of black velvet round the throat, of which the French women are so fond. I am sure I did not see an ugly woman in Quebec, nor one that, to my eye, was not sensibly and prettily habited, and such little fat loves of children, chattering French with their nurses. The people were as picturesque as the place, and nobody scrutinized you as they do in New York, fixing a stony stare upon you (I speak of the New York women), till they have found out everything you have on, how it is made and trimmed, and then comment upon the same to their next elbow neighbor. Every healthy and contented-looking female soul of them seemed to have business of their own, and to mind it. Now and then, to be sure, an officer or a private would take a look in passing, and sometimes we heard them say "Anglice," and that is where they did not hit it, at least with the ladies of the party, spite of light hair and eyes. A gentleman at the hotel where we stayed, said, "Those ladies are English," looking at myself and daughter. English! when we talked and laughed, ate and drank, got up and sat down, without ever once looking into a book of etiquette to see if it was "proper!"

A drive, which I shall long remember, we took to a little French village just out of Quebec. I had always thought—shade of Napoleon, forgive me—

that the peasant French were an unthrifty, unneat people. My delight was unbounded at their rows of neat little white-washed cottages, standing sociably and cosily together, with long strips of farms extending back; not an unsightly object about them; clean, white-muslin window-curtains, with pretty pots of bright, flowering plants at the casements; rosy little children, with their bright red stockings—how I *like* to see a little child in red stockings—and clean, white aprons, and shiny hair, sitting on the door-step with the family Towser, or running after the carriage, with bunches of flowers for "the English ladies," as they persisted in calling us, keeping up with our horses with a pertinacity which would have drawn out the pennies were we less favorably inclined; and gay little bouquets they gave us, too—roses just in bloom (for their summers are late and fleeting), and pretty pinks and geranium leaves. In the fields, women and girls were raking hay, with broad straw hats, which they pushed back from their brown faces, as they leaned on their rakes to look as we passed, quite unconscious how pretty they looked, helping their stout, healthy-looking brothers, who, with strong, white teeth, and curly hair, laughed merrily as they tossed the hay about. And yet this, like all pictures, had its shadow, for *I* saw, though they did not, the pale procession of half-paid sewing girls coming up Nassau and Chatham streets, in New York, at that very moment, home to some stifled attic, or perhaps some more noisome place, of which those Canadians, in their pure country seclusion, could not even dream. How I wished they were all in those sweet hayfields, breathing that pure, untainted air!

Oh, it was a delicious picture; I could have looked at it forever; and at every turn in the road some lovely view enchanted us—some new blending of sea and sky, wood and valley, and each perfect of its kind; and so we came at last to the famous Falls of "Montmorenci," where we were to have twenty-five cents' worth of a miniature Niagara, with root-beer and sponge-cake "to suit," for an additional fee; and truly they might have been more extortionate as far as the Falls were concerned, were it not such a damper to sentiment to pay for one's ecstasy by the shilling. Beautiful were the Falls, tumbling, dashing, and foaming down into their rocky bed beneath, where were patches of velvet moss, of as vivid a green as your foot ever sank in while wandering in the cool, fragrant woods. Of course we were pointed to the remains of the "suspension bridge," which, about four years ago, broke so treacherously over the Falls, precipitating a whole family to instant death in the boiling torrent below. A great, hungry monster it looked to us after that, as we went shuddering up the steep steps to sunlight and safety, after viewing it from below. "Not one of them was ever heard of, I suppose?" said I to our boy guide. "Not one, ma'am," replied my juvenile oracle, with a solemn sniffle that would have done credit to a camp-meeting.

Oh, these early breakfasts in "banquet halls deserted" of huge hotels, waited upon by yawning servants scarce awake; no appetite for the food you know you will be dying for five or six hours afterwards; meanwhile, conscious only of an intense and unmitigated disgust for big trunks, little trunks, bonnet-boxes, keys, carpet-bags, and reticules. The morning foggy and chill; the hotel parlor, so pleasant the evening before, as you sat upon its comfortable sofa with a party of friends looking now quite as miserable as you feel, with its gay bouquets of yesterday drooping and faded. Blue-looking men emerging from the bar-room, twisting their travelling-shawls, in folds more warm than graceful, over their chests and shoulders; ladies shivering as the chill morning air strikes their but half-protected, shrinking figures. "All ready" at last, and away we start for Portland. Yet, stay; what's this? Heaven bless that ebony waiter, who, running after me, slid into my hand a cold chicken, with a little package of salt inclosed, and with an indescribable twist of his good-natured, shiny phiz, whispers, "Ladies gets *so* hungry on railroads, ma'am!" Now that's what I call a compliment, and a substantial one, too; he should have seen me a few hours after with one of the drumsticks, bless his soul. May he meet some appreciative Dinah, and may they never want for a chicken!

Rain, rain, rain all day, in the most pitiless manner. Some solace themselves with newspapers, some with novels, and some with sleep; the latter sure to be broken in upon by the conductor's nudge, and "your ticket, sir!" Directly in front of me sat two young men, strangers to each other, who presently finding one of those convenient pretexts for speaking which travel always affords, commenced conversation. Imagine how long those two fellows kept it up without stopping to wink, or even to look at the "way-stations"! *Sixty-five miles!*— I repeat it—*sixty-five miles!* Wouldn't the fact have been published from Dan to Beersheba, had the conversationists happened to have been a couple of women? And by the help of the limitless NEW YORK LEDGER, I'll send it thus far. Mostly, these young men appeared to pity the Canadian nuns, whom they seemed to have philanthropic desires to benefit, without the opportunity. Then the vexed question of North and South was discussed, that grindstone upon which every youngster must needs whet his jack-knife. But time would fail to tell all the nonsense I was forced, in the next seat, to hear, far transcending that of women, which, the saints know, is ofttimes bad enough.

Well, we lived through that day's drizzle and rain, and reached Portland in a most limp condition, just at night. Curious to be again in a birthplace which I left when I was but six weeks old! "If the sun will only shine out to-morrow," said I, as I cuddled under the blankets with horrible forebodings. The fates were propitious. A warm, lovely morning; every tree and shrub newly polished, and as fresh as if just made. Within range of my window was a beautiful garden, gay as a rainbow with all sorts of brilliant flowers. Two Quakers came along in solemn drab. I smiled and held my breath. "Thank God," said I, as I saw them lean delightedly over the fence to look at the gay flowers, "nature is, and ever will be, stronger than creeds." A hasty breakfast, and forth I started on my exploring tour. "I shall know the house where I was born, if I pass it," said I; "some magnetic influence will surely arrest my steps. Stay, that is Dr. Payson's church." "How do you know?" asked my companions. "I *feel* it; ask and see." And so it was. He who, by his sweet, consistent, loving, holy life, came between me and the grim creed which my very soul spurned, and which was driving me to disbelieve all of which his Christ-like life was the beautiful exponent. *He* who laid holy hands of blessing on my baby-forehead, and knew God's creatures too well to try to drive them, through fear of endless torment, to heaven. I felt like crossing myself, as I passed the church where his feet had so often entered, to tell, in that most musical of voices, of God's infinite love to everything He had made—of God's infinite pity— but why attempt to convey an idea of what must have been heard to be understood and felt? Hundreds whom man's denunciatory self-righteousness had driven to cursing, bitterness, and despair, are now stars in his crown.

Well, I passed on through the lovely streets of my native city, with their green hedges and climbing plants, and bright flowers, and stately trees, and most substantial, palatial stone houses, with shining window-panes and massive entrances. Not there, not there, said I; it must have been in some small wooden house, with an inch or two of ground, and perhaps a few flowers that needed little care, for those were humble days to her who, taking the baby-boy (poet that was to be) in her arms, went daily to nurse him in the jail where his father was confined. She who, if there *is* a heaven of bliss, is in it to-day, as one of those earth-martyrs whose mask of heavenly serenity a short-sighted world never pierces. No, I feel no throb at my heart when looking at these grand houses. Sure I am, it was not there that the baby was baptized, whose little grave-clothes were well nigh bespoken. It was not there that the little face purpled with what they said was the death-agony. Would to God it had pleased Him to make it so. It was not there that the little life began, from which that baby might well struggle to escape. And so, wearily my feet passed up and down one lovely street after another, admiring all, yet not drawn magnetically to any. *Somewhere*—let it suffice—in that lovely, leafy city, with its grand old drooping elms, and glimpses of the broad, blue sea, I first opened eyes that will close far enough away from its Sabbath stillness and quiet.

IDLE HOURS AT OUR OWN EMERALD ISLE, THE GEM OF THE SEA.

DON'T you wish you were here in Newport with me? the broad, blue ocean in front of your window, and the crisp sea-breeze sending fresh life through every vein? For a while we shall have Newport mostly to ourselves, as at this present writing Fashion still lingers in the city, searching for dry-goods to do this lovely spot fitting honor, according to their idea of the same. Meantime we look at their lovely gardens and velvety lawns, adorned like a bride for her expectant spouse, and bewitching, with their flowery contrasts of vivid color, beyond any words I can find to express them. Hanging baskets of ivy and scarlet geranium, swinging like the censers of the Catholic churches, and diffusing incense as we pass. Now and then some little white-robed child springs out upon a door-step, with a frame of vine leaves above her lovely, unconscious head, and the picture is complete. She will never, in after years, have a more fervent worshipper at her feet than I, at that moment. Turn where you will in Newport, all is beauty. If you weary of the finish and elegance of these beautiful villas, there is the rocky shore, where the sea dashes with tireless vigor; or you can contemplate the bay that lies sparkling in the sunlight; or you can walk or ride in the many lovely roads which give wonderfully beautiful glimpses of both, and are as much "country" in their leafy and quiet seclusion, as if Fashion were exiled to the North Pole, instead of the distance of a mile or so. Then, if you are book-y, there are the well-stocked libraries of the place; and for ladies whose shopping propensities no raging dog-star allays or hinders, stores, where New York and other cities have freely poured out their knicknacks, in the shape of ribbons, dress goods, laces, and—dearer than all—"*embroidery worsted!*"

Think of the blasphemy of using this last, when nature has so far outrivalled them! I wonder they are not afraid of being struck with lightning for such presumption. But nobody knows the coquetry lurking in a skein of bright worsted, held in lily, diamond-decked fingers, in the corner of a vine-wreathed piazza. I declare that I will turn "state's evidence," and expose it. *Blue* worsted now, in the hands of a sunny-haired, white-robed blonde; crimson or yellow on the lap of a dark-haired brunette! And *you*, simple Theodore or Frank, never dreaming that these effects are studied with the nicest diplomatic skill by these "artless" creatures at whose feet you are willing slaves. Whatsoever you do, don't offer to hold one of those skeins for winding. That brings heads, and fingers, too, together in a manner—well, don't you do it, that's all. Offer to kill caterpillars, if you will, or rose-bugs; that's a safe employment; but in this worsted business, take my word for it, you will be sure to get worsted yourself. It is quite safe, however, for you to drive with them, if they invite you, in those cunning little phaetons with the footman at your back, because flirting in that case is under difficulties, not easily conquered unless you lose him off upon the road. Meantime Newport remains the gem of summer seaside resorts, combining, as it does, society or seclusion at your pleasure, and city and country, with all the advantages of both.

If you only knew the delicious laziness that has taken possession of me this bird-singing morning, you wouldn't poke me up to write. A soft mist half veils the ocean, so turbulent last night, and butterflies in pairs are wooing, now in the vines about my window, then darting out into the bright meadows for a longer flight. I am fascinated with the graceful circles they make. I am fascinated with that old cow, too indolent even to whisk the flies off her back, standing as she has stood for an hour under that big tree. I love to see the pretty maidens, with their fresh young faces and saucy little hats, driving their cunning ponies past my window. Now and then comes borne to my ear by this soft west wind a child's silvery laugh, as musical as the ripple of a brook. I am away, thank Heaven, from "riots" and murder, save in the chicken line; and I hope nobody will debate "female suffrage" with me to-day, or ask my opinion on anything, save the heavenliness of this beautiful Newport, where the daily delightful surprises of Nature, by land and ocean, keep me in a constant state of beatitude. Now and then I get wroth with the over-dressed dames, who evidently have no eyes for it, or appreciation of it, save to strike attitudes on the soft green lawn, or lounge elegantly in the fashionable drive, with poodle and baby and husband and carriage robe, arranged like a tableau to be gazed at; never driving where it is dusty, for fear of the sacred dry-goods, though Nature woo ever so sweetly. Talk of the "laboring classes"! The amount of "labor" these women will take upon themselves in the languid summer days is past my computation. I encountered one in a shop here the other day, trailing after her, at eleven in the morning, a wonderful length of silk robe, and wringing her tightly kidded fingers because a particular kind of ribbon was not to be had, and with a gesture of despair exclaiming, "I must telegraph instantly to New York for it." Poor thing! I say *poor* advisedly. I had rather be the barefooted, blithe little girl who drives the cows home, if I had to make my choice. What is woman without a shop? Storekeepers here act on this principle, and spread their lures accordingly. Not that ladies go to buy always, but it is a sort of Exchange, where their toilets can be displayed, as well as a neat ankle, while alighting from a gay carriage at the door.

I think there are more *Stars* in Newport than in any other place. There was a wonderful profusion out last evening. Not literary stars—though Newport is full of them too, if the crazy kind of abstracted, *author* look is any indication. Flowing hair upon the coat collar, and a scarlet bit of necktie, and general sauciness of dress and demeanor, are generally indicative of an artist. *I* find no fault. Give us individuality, or give us death. This world would be a sorry place without it. There are worse people than " queer people " about. The queerest I ever met, was a woman who prided herself on her surpassing ugliness, and dressed up to the character, selecting always those colors which intensified it. I am happy to state that her husband was a match for her in this respect. But so witty was she, that no young beauty at the hotel had so many followers and admirers. I really think she enjoyed her own hideousness. After hearing her witticisms, you would go your way and remember it no more, or if so, only to admire the wisdom of her conquest over it.

Yes, I am idle here. But that reminds me—is anything more diverting than the advice so lavishly tendered to women as to the " best mode of passing their time in the country, during the summer months"?

One writer recommends that " they should take up the study of a new language." That sounds well; but suppose a lady to have been a teacher all the rest of the year? This would scarcely be an exhilarating, restful occupation. Another wonders that " some one lady does not read aloud to a group of lady friends." That sounds well too; but some ladies like history, others biography; many, indiscriminate novels. Then how few, even among so-called "educated" ladies, read well, or, reading well, have power to read aloud for any length of time; or, these points being favorable, can bring the other women to a focus as to the hour agreed upon, or keep them at it, when they get them there, without frequent yawning, unless, indeed, a gentleman be included in the party! Some, again, propose "botany" to them; and there are ladies who, preferring health to dry-goods, carry out this advice successfully. As to the study of botany, for one, I would rather call fox-glove fox-glove, than to call it *fox a borondibus ora gloribundus!* but then that is a matter of taste and breath. I should be much more likely also to look at its shape and coloring, than to search the encyclopædia for its horticultural baptism. But then, as an eminent biographer is apt to remark to me fifty times a day, "That's a peculiarity of *yours*, Fanny." Who said it wasn't? Haven't I a right to my peculiarities, as has a tree to its shape and foliage, and blossoms and fruit? And while we are in the leafy line, why isn't a Fern as good as any other kind of grass? I've seen pretty tall ferns in my day, especially up the Shaker road, a little out of Stockbridge, Mass., where, I have no doubt, they are waving in plumy luxuriance at this very minute.

This is a digression; but you would digress too,

had you ever ridden that road of a bright summer day.

To return to my subject. Wholesale giving of advice, on this or any other point, is like administering medicine; none but quacks give it without considering constitutional tendencies, as well as the age and daily habits of the patient. Unfortunately, with advice-givers these points are generally ignored: one and the same pill being supposed remedial for all times, seasons, and complaints, especially where women are concerned, who really need more classifying than any big lump of men who were ever thrown together—such infinite variety and delicate shading is there in their mental, moral, and physical make-up. But of this, man is either wilfully or indifferently ignorant, since he never mentions the subject without committing egregious blunders.

I never hear a man remark, "*you women!*" that I don't mentally send him "*to the foot of the class.*"

"*You* women!" Why, a man may live with even *one* woman all his life, and yet really know no more about her, than I do why men were born at all. I heard a husband once deplore that, being ignorant of the French language, he could not know the meaning of a sentence in the book he was reading.

"Give it to me," replied his wife, immediately translating it. "Why," exclaimed he, in astonishment, "I never knew you understood French!" And yet he had lived with her fifteen years. It is just so with other and still more important knowledge of a wife. Now I ask you, Mr. BONNER, when you choose a horse, if you do not first find out what that horse can do, especially how fast he can trot without damage?—which, by the way, is the last question a married man thinks of asking about his wife.

Well, isn't a wife quite as important an animal as a horse? I would like to see *Dexter* put to dragging stones on the highway, or *Pocahontas* to rotary sawing of wood at a railway station!

And yet thousands of men all over the country make stupider blunders than these about their wives, every day in the year, partly, as I say, through ignorance, which of course is culpable, and partly through indifference.

Many women, if they were half as judiciously managed, as to their physical needs and possible capabilities, as are horses, would be worth much more to their owners; and I am sure I have seen men to whom this argument would be the only one they would think worth listening to. Also, in all fairness, I should add, that I have seen others who remembered it first and always.

SOME CITY SIGHTS.

MORE than in any other locality does a funeral passing through Broadway seem impressive to me. There, while life is at the flood, and thousands pass and repass you whose faces you do not recognize, save by the universal stamp of eagerness and bustle and hurry, as if the goal in the distance which they aim at was for eternity and not for fleeting time; there, where bright eyes shine brightest, and silken locks and silken dresses shimmer fairest in the dancing sunbeams; there, where all nations, all interests are represented, and the panorama never halts, day or night, but only substitutes one set of moving figures for another; there, indeed, does Death *seem* Death when it glides stealthily in among the busy, surging crowd.

Once, walking there on a bright sunny day, I met four pall-bearers, slowly bearing a coffin covered with black, with the clergyman in his gown and bands, and the mourners following. Instinctively the gay crowd parted upon the sidewalk, the men standing with uncovered heads; the laugh died upon the lips of the young girl; the little children looked on, wondering and awe-struck. Even she over whose own grave no loving tear might ever fall, bowed her defiant head, and for one brief moment faced that terrible thought. And so the slow procession passed, though no one knew who slept so quietly amid all that din and noise; but knowing only that some heart, some home was desolate. Then the eager crowd closed in again, and new faces passed smilingly, new forms stepped gayly, smart equipages dashed by, and the jest and the laugh fell again upon my ear as before, while I seemed to move as one in a dream.

Once again, but in the country, fragrant with blossoms, and sweet with the song of birds and the murmured whisper of leaves, just such a sombre procession crossed the green fields, under the blue sky, with its quiet burden. It is long years since I witnessed both; but they stand out in my memory, each as distinctly as if it were but yesterday. I don't know which was the more impressive. I only know that when I looked upon the latter, I said to myself, when life's fret is over, just so would *I* be carried to my last rest.

One of the prettiest sights to be seen in the early morning is that of the little girls going to school. I like them best of a rainy day, because then their sweet little faces beam from out little close hoods, drawn about their red cheeks; and their little fat calves have such a tussle with the wind as they try to get round gusty corners; so that what with battling with their sandwich-boxes, and what with their geographies, their gleaming white teeth make a very lovely show between their rosy lips. What policeman, with the heart of a father, but would rather help a flock of these pretty birds across the street than a bevy of paniered ladies who shrink from their touch, all the while they are ready to scream with fright if they are *not* taken by the arm.

Commend me to the little girls of six, eight, and twelve, who, not yet having come to their wickedness, squeal out with delicious frankness, "Mr. Policeman! Mr. Policeman! please come carry me over the street." And so they swarm round him like a cloud of bees till they are all safely landed on the other side.

Bless their little innocent faces! It is as good as a chapter of the Bible to any policeman, to see such sweet white lilies blossoming amid the physical and moral filth which they meet in their rounds in the New York streets.

As it is rather an exception to find a little school-*boy* who is not either a little saintly prig or a little well-dressed ruffian and bully, I have not contemplated their goings and comings with the same satisfaction as I do that of their little sisters; though *why* a little *boy* shouldn't be as well-mannered as a little girl I have always been at a loss to know.

One is occasionally an eye-witness to scenes in New York which momentarily paralyze one's faith in humanity, I had almost said in God. One lovely afternoon of last week I determined to try the drive by the "new Hudson River road to Fort Lee," which, by the way, I rapturously commend, *en passant*, to every New Yorker, and stranger within our gates who is fond of beautiful scenery. On the way we alighted, and entered one of the numerous rural gardens, to enjoy from thence a fine view of the river. Immediately our attention was arrested by loud voices; among which we distinguished that of a woman, now in loud, angry tones, then soft and pleading, as if deprecating personal violence. "Pay up, then," vociferated a coarse, masculine voice, as a stout man appeared, grasping a young girl of eighteen or twenty by the wrist, dressed in a soiled tawdry bonnet and silk gown, and forcibly ejected her from the piazza of a refreshment room into the garden. She was a woman and young, and without understanding her offence, his brutality roused me; but my blood froze in my veins, when gathering up her form to its full height, raising her small hand in the air, and flashing her dark eyes, she cursed him as only a woman *can* curse who is lost for this world and the next. And men stood by and heard it, who had mothers and sisters, and laughed, and jeered, and maddened her already excited blood, *for sport,* to fiercer words of unwomanly strife! A young man of her own age, who appeared to have accompanied her there, and seemed terrified at the turn of affairs, stepped to her side; but she sprang upon him like a panther, then bounded past him, then seized a garden stool, and hurling it at his head with blistering curses, ran through the garden to the river. For the first time I found voice to say—Great God—she will drown herself! and before the words were out of my mouth—a leap—a splash—and she had disappeared. A boat was near, into which two men jumped, and succeeded with her companion in catching hold of her dress, after she had twice sunk. Pale, gasping, in her tawdry, dripping finery, she was dragged on shore. One of the men turning to her companion said, "another twenty-five cents due for fishing her out." Then two or three men—I suppose they *called* themselves men—took her under the arm-pits with her face downward, and two went behind and seized her by the heels, her drapery falling back from her knees, while other men of the same stamp walked behind gazing at her exposed limbs. Then they laid her upon a garden bench with her white face upturned to the fair sky, and stood over the gasping, sobbing creature, with less feeling than they would gaze upon a maimed horse or dog; her dress, torn from her neck, revealing to their beastly gaze youth and beauty which God never made for this desecration.

Oh! could I by a word have summoned the advocates of *Free Love* to that spot—then and there would I have given them my dumb, eloquent answer to their nauseous, hell-begotten doctrines. I would have summoned thither those women who have lately stood up in public as champions of their sex's "rights" (Heaven defend us from their polluted, polluting tongues), and bade them look upon what they *must* know to be the inevitable end of promiscuous "affinity." I would have summoned there those men of position in the community, who sit in their carpeted, well-stocked library, and in full view of their household gods—within sound of the innocent prattle of their own children—by their own *yet* undesecrated hearthstones—write fine-spun theories upon Free-Love, claiming for its brazen female advocates the title of "modest" women! I would have summoned thither the editors of those respectable daily journals, who publish in their columns the sophistical effusions of such men, and bade them, one and all, look upon that young, gasping girl, and the coarse men who stood by and jeered at her.

As I turned soul-sick away, I saw a woman standing at a little distance with an infant in her arms, her face white with fear. As she gave a last glance at the girl she pressed her babe convulsively to her breast and covered its innocent face with kisses. The action was suggestive. Alas, just so must that lost young girl's mother *once* have kissed *her!*

How Easy to Say "be Cheerful"!—"Be cheerful," says the man who is easy in his circumstances, missing no loved face at the table, nor by the hearth. But does he ever consider how hard it may be to be "cheerful" when the heart aches, and the cupboard is empty, and there are little fresh graves in the church-yard, and friends are few or indifferent, and even God, for the time being, seems to have forgotten us, so desolate is our lot? How difficult for one man to understand another, in such different circumstances! How easy to *say*, "Be cheerful!" How hard he would find it to practise it, were *he* stripped of all life's brightness!

DOG-DAYS IN THE MOUNTAINS.

TO whomsoever human nature is a pleasant study, I would recommend as an inviting field a summer boarding-place. Wood, rocks, and lakes are nothing beside human nature. We can form some sort of an idea on geological, aquarian, and other principles, why *they* exist. We quite indorse the Scriptural statement at creation that they are all "very good." But I am puzzled to know why a woman who can do nothing but simper and fold her hands should be married and have children without number, and another beneath whose large motherly heart no little one ever has or ever will nestle, should go mourning all her days on account of it. Why a man whose every impulse and feeling and purpose are unswervingly in the right direction should have an empty pocket; and a mean, narrow-minded, ignorant, miserable apology for a man, have his tight fist on a full one. Why consumptives and scrofulous people should insist on industriously increasing the census, and men and women made physically on the right principles pertinaciously cling to celibacy. Why the serving-maid should have more womanliness, intelligence, and goodness, than the mistress whose irate voice makes her tremble. Why the clergyman should pay such undeviating attention to the *soul* of his child that he cannot spare time to see that his body at twelve years of age is "standing from under." Why a man marries a woman merely for her beauty, and is disgusted in two weeks that she has not turned out an intellectual companion. Why a good man, but *not* an *intellectual* one, marries a "strong-minded woman," and instantly sets about teaching her that obedience and silence are the first duties of wives. Why young men should decline marriage on the score that "they cannot afford it," when they spend more than would support a family, on their vices. Why a man with the proportions of Hercules should have a voice like a squeaking door-hinge, and a lovely girl deafen you every time she opens her rosebud mouth. In short, why, when men and women are such natural curiosities—singly or in groups, married or celibate—should showmen, at such cost of outlay, stock their premises with anacondas and giraffes, when their fellow-critters "would be so rich" an exhibition?

But think as long and as industriously as I may on these vexed questions, no solution comes. I turn them over to some philosopher who will unravel the skein while I take an evening sail upon the lake. In fact, when I get *there*, I don't care what becomes of my kind so that my sunset sail is not denied me. Nor is this as selfish as it seems, since I should not be safe company for them in the dog-days without this soothing process. Keep close to the shore now, oh, boatman: and above all, keep silence. Pickerel are good in their way, but bony; and I would fain listen dreamily to the plashing oar, and the twit-twit of the little birds as they seek their nests in the trees, while my eye rests on the changing clouds and their reflections in the smooth mirror below. Vex me not with talk of "dead swells" and "whitecaps." I would sail here till midnight in silence, and thence straight into the other world, before a ripple of earthly fret came over my spirit.

But it is not to be. One of our party "wants to pick pond-lilies," slimy and smell-less; *not* like the dear old pond-lilies in Massachusetts, though mockingly like in form and color. Another is yelling at an echo, which answers back as persistently as if it were of the feminine gender; but, unlike the feminine gender, always *agrees* colloquially. Another pokes me up from my reverie to know "why I am so stupid?" And now when the shadows are loveliest and the moon beginning to silver the lake, the universal voice is "to land." Let them go. Good riddance! Two of us stay with the boatman. Now flash up the Northern lights! Now appears the evening star, crowning yonder hill, and twinkling defiantly in the very face of the new moon. Plucky star! That's right! to take for your motto that of America—*Room and freedom for all.*

"What will we *ever* do when we get back to New York?" dolefully asked little Bright Eyes of me, the other day, as she came in with her apron full of mosses and flowers. That's just it. That's what *I* want to know. No cool lake awaits me there at eventide, on whose broad expanse one can float into serenity. But instead, gas-lighted, unventilated public assemblies, where vexed questions are agitated: and in place of bird-singing, inodorous streets, full of children whose "childhood" is a myth. And for the lovely fresh morning, with its aromatic odors, the whoop of milkmen, the rush of street cars, and the old mälstrom whirl of business, folly, and sin. My very soul sickens to think of it. I *won't* think of it. I'll lay off and dream.

Every summer vacation I ask myself, why people who have no relish for country life doom themselves to yawn through six or eight weeks of it? People who never move from a certain chair on the piazza save to migrate to their beds, or to the dining-table; who have neither eyes to see earth's glory, nor heart to be grateful for it, or ears open to its myriad musical voices—living discords amid all its harmony. If invalids, I can understand and pity their misfortune; but your fat, well-to-do, buxom men and women, who have no earthly impediment to their locomotion, and yet who live weeks in the vicinity of grand natural objects, and are just as dead to them as the ox in the meadow—why do they travel thousands of dusty miles to get to them? People who look pityingly at you, as you return exhilarated from your delicious rambles, as if to say, "*Poor lunatics!*" One turns from them to the children, to whom every daisy and blade of grass is a bright heaven, and counts sadly over their lost years. Also,

I would like to ask, is there anything in the climate of Vermont which turns out such huge trees, mountains, and *men*, that dwarfs nearly all its womankind? Again: Do preserves and pills, flap-jacks and ipecac, plum-cake and castor-oil, jelly and jalap have a natural affinity, that they are so often found in each other's company? In other words: Why do the country-women of New England waste their time in concocting the indigestible richness which everybody is better without, and which renders these drugs necessary? Half the time thus spent, if devoted to the manufactory of that rare commodity—sweet, wholesome bread—or to the best way of cooking meat so as to preserve its juices, would shut up the drug-shops, prolong their own lives and good looks, and make them a credit to the glorious country in which they are born. *Give us good bread*, my dear country-women. What else soever you pass over, *don't slight the bread*. It is the crying sin of the country, that if there are cakes and pies in plenty, the bread may be sour, or filled with saleratus, or so stale that a dog would not swallow it, or so "slack-baked" that one might as well eat dough. Now the digestion of an ostrich would fail on such fare as this. A healthy stomach revolts at it, and refuses to be put off with sweets and preserves. It is a crime to set such bread before *little children*, even if adult digestion were equal to it, which it is not. A great reform is needed here, and if I can help it on, I care not who boxes my ears for the attempt. To see human beings making and swallowing such messes, and then sending physic after it, like a detective, to clear it from the system, is a proceeding which should give them all a free pass to the Lunatic Asylum. There—now I feel better! While I am catechising, do you suppose there was ever an invalid who didn't button-hole everybody, to recapitulate his or her symptoms, exhibit their tongues, and discuss patent medicines? It gets monotonous after a while, particularly when you know that they are bound personally to experiment on every pill, powder, and plaster that any heartless quack may invent to make a living. If half of them were to stop taking physic entirely, live on wholesome food, take plenty of fresh air and sleep, they would never know pain or ache. Don't the doctors know this, and laugh in their sleeves at it? And *does a doctor ever give drugs to his own family?* I think I have asked questions enough for the present, so we will consider the meeting adjourned.

SPRING IN THE CITY.

THERE are those who like to begin the day vociferously; with demonstrative step and voice; with hurry and rush. I confess to a love of the serene, soft-stepping way in which Nature heralds in the day. Soft skies, softer music; the gradual rolling up of night's mantle, and the genial warmth which steals imperceptibly about us. Oh, that sweet, quiet, devotional coming in of the newborn day! How I long for it, as the blades of grass begin to grow green, between the pavement-stones of the crazy city! How I tire of its quips and pranks and circus-clown-tumblings. How stale grow its jests! How I pant for freedom outside its artificial, heated walls! How disgusting is the road woman must travel to secure all this happiness! Woollens and furs to be put safely out of reach of moths. House-cleaning and carpet-shaking to be done. Dresses to be bought, and horror! worse than all, to be fitted. Trunks to be packed—writing to be done, weeks ahead. My brain spins to think what a purgatory one must travel through, to reach that serene heaven, the bird-peeping-morning-hour of the country; when nobody comes to me with horrible questions about meat and butter. When as soon as my shoes and stockings are on, and before the dew is off, or the lovely mist done creeping off the mountains, Nature's cool hand is laid on my temples, and I give *her* the best of me. With my head on her bosom, I forget all that is askew in life and rest there contented with the present; like the babe who dreams not that its mother will presently loose its hand from her neck, and disappear while yet the trance continues.

If I am sentimental, forgive me; but sometimes I sigh to think how much of life goes to consideration of food and clothes. Now, while I sojourned in a tent on the James river, during the war, I used to lie in my cot, and consider these things among others. There were just the cot, a rough pine table, and my trunk, for furniture. I had only to wash my face and hands in the tin basin of water that Sambo slipped under the tent every morning, and all those bothering, small considerations were disposed of for the day.

There was no carpet there to be swept—there were no pictures or china to look after. Sambo made my bed, while I went into another tent to breakfast; and the fighting was going on outside, which was to leave it optional with Sambo about handing tin-basins of water to white folks. All that suited me. Life under these circumstances seemed to have something in it. I felt dignified to be alive, and thanked my father and mother for it.

We have finished the war since then. I am not sorry for that, but life in that tent has spoiled me for parlor fripperies. That's the worst of it. I keep all the time asking everybody if they don't think we should be a great deal happier without all these artificial wants, that so wear our spirits and souls out. Bless you, they all say, yes; but they keep going on all the same, and I suppose I shall.

A WOMAN'S MOTION.—I rise to make a proposition. It is this: that the name and denomination, and the name of the pastor, of our respective churches, should be neatly placed beside the principal entrance door, that strangers may be able to find those churches they desire. Why not? as well as the name of the sexton and his residence, which we find upon nearly all our churches. I won't charge anything for the hint, provided it is carried out. The thought came to me as I was touched upon the arm by a stranger the other Sunday, in the porch of a New York church, and asked, "Of what denomination is the pastor here?" I had to rub my head to remember, for creeds and denominations find little lodgment there. Provided I find Christianity, that's enough for me, and to my thinking, no one church has the monopoly of that.

WAIFS.

DID you ever try to rid yourself of a thing you did not want? An old glove or a faded knot of ribbon, or a bit of lace? After Bettina has picked it up, and with honest delight returned it as a missing valuable, and every adult and minor in the house has taken his or her turn in depositing it carefully on your table, were you ever driven "clean" demented by the dust-man ringing the area bell, with the article in question, thinking, deluded philanthropist, that he had performed a virtuous action? Go where you may, can you rid yourself of it? Don't it turn up between the covers of books, and stare at you from bureau drawers, and appear simultaneously with your pocket-handkerchief on some august occasion from your robe pocket? Will water quench it, or fire burn it? Don't it always fly up chimney unharmed by the sparks, and watch an opportunity to re-enter at the area door? When you go out, don't it frisk along the gutter, timing itself to your steps, slow or quick; or eddy round your head in a gust of wind, and finally get blown back upon your door-step, where it persists in lodging, spite of brooms and Bettys, till you get as nervous about it as if it were some relentless enemy, dogging your every step? Perhaps all this while you are hunting every nook and corner vainly to find some article you *really* want, and which persistently keeps out of your way, or at least until you have given it up, and replaced it with a duplicate, when it takes that occasion suddenly to appear, and innocently to confront you, from a fold in an arm-chair, or sofa, or from the corner of a carpet.

When I experience these trials, I no longer marvel at the clutching fingers thrust through the grated windows of lunatic asylums, or the unearthly howls of rage or peals of wild laughter with which these unfortunates give vent to their feelings. I no longer smile at the annoyed man who, waking one fine spring morning, and looking at the fresh grass, exclaimed, " What! *Green again!* and—*blue*—his brains (?) out."

PARTIAL JUDGMENT.—How few people are gifted with the faculty of seeing round a corner; in other words, looking at both sides of a question before deciding! Those who have *not* this gift are always sinning, and always repenting; always asserting, and always retracting. They may have many estimable qualities, and yet, their house being built on such a sandy foundation, one hesitates before entering it; or, if he makes up his mind to do so, it is with the deliberate expectation that he may possibly be buried under its ruins.

TACT.

I'M not particularly good at definitions, but I know what tact is not. It is nót tact to sit down by the side of a person grieving for the dead, and tell them how much more comfortable life would now be to them, did they not love so strongly; and how much wiser, could they only be more diffusive in their attachments, and concentrate less; so that when the crape flutters from the door, one could coolly say: "Yes, it is true—he or she is dead and gone; and there's no help for it; let us turn to something else and be jolly."

It is not tact to tell a mother, who has an idiotic or deformed child, how smart, and sweet, and bright are your own; with what a zest they enter into rollicksome sports; how apt they are to learn, and how brilliant may be their own and your future.

It is not tact, if you have an acquaintance, who only by the most rigid and painstaking economy can maintain a presentable appearance, to make a call on such, in an elaborate toilet, with manners to match.

It is not tact to embarrass persons of limited education, and little reading, by conversing upon topics of which they can by no possibility know anything, save that you have the advantage of them in that regard. It is not tact, in the presence of an invalid, to dilate upon savory dishes, and the pleasures of the table. It is not tact to converse with an editor upon a quiet, peaceful life; or with a compelled authoress upon the safe and uninvaded sanctities of the fireside for women.

The most astounding instance of *tact*, is to listen, inwardly crucified, with a pleased air, to an old—*old* joke, and a poor one at that: to improvise a laugh at the proper moment, and successfully to resist the malicious instinct to flatter the narrator, at the close, by saying: "Yes, I have heard that before."

ANSWER YOUR CHILDREN'S QUESTIONS.—Education is erroneously supposed only to be had at schools. The most ignorant children often have been constant in their attendance there, and there have been very intelligent ones who never saw the inside of a school-room. The child who always asks an explanation of terms or phrases it cannot understand, who is never willing to repeat, parrot-like, that which is incomprehensible, will far outstrip in "education" the ordinary routine scholar. "Education" goes on with children at the fireside—on the street—at church—at play—everywhere. Do not refuse to answer their proper questions then. Do not check this natural intelligence, for which *books* can never compensate, though you bestowed whole libraries.

THE INFIRMITIES OF GENIUS.

"POOR Burns!" all exclaim after reading his life and his poems. Poor Burns! *I* too say; and the next minute I ask, impatiently, why *he*, so conscious of his God-given powers, should have miserably shortened his life one-half by ill-governed appetites and excesses. Why, if coining his brain into dollars, for the widow and fatherless, proved impossible, he should become so disgusted with manual labor, that even his filial, fraternal, and conjugal love could not dignify its repulsive features, since it needs *must be*. Why, with a loving, prudent, industrious, faithful wife to help him, he could not emulate her everyday but sublime heroism, not by paroxysms of effort, only to show us how well he *might* have done, but that steady, determined persistence which seldom fails of success. Why he, at once so great and so little, took pleasure and pride in wallowing in the mire, merely because strait-laced hypocrisy stepped daintily over it with white-sandalled feet. There was no greatness in this. It was but the angry kick of the impatient urchin upon the chair over which he had stumbled. Did his ambition to be written down a publican and a sinner lessen the ranks of the Pharisee? Could he look into the trusting faces of his innocent children, and feel no secret pang that for so petty and unworthy a motive he was content to hazard or forego their future respect? Had he none but himself to consult in such unworthy disposition of his time and talents? Was it *manly* in the midst of that loving group coolly to look forward to the possibility of an old age of beggary, and toleration by chance firesides, in the undignified character of jester or clown? Because a man is a "genius," must one indorse these things and write them down as "eccentricities" inseparable from it and to be lightly passed over? Must intellect *necessarily* be at variance with principle?

And yet—and yet—because I can say this, I do not fall a whit behind the most ardent admirer of his genius. But I *do* hold that he is to be held as accountable for his errors as the most ordinary farmer's boy who is unable to spell the name of the plough which he guides. Nor does this interfere with the heart-aching pity with which I look upon the soiled wings, so capable of soaring into a pure atmosphere, yet trailing their beauty in the dust. Nor does this keep my eyes from overflowing when some lofty or beautiful sentiment of his shines out diamond-like from the rubbish.

How could he? Why did he?

Softly—reverently let us answer. We so full of faults—always sinning—sometimes repenting. Softly let us answer. We who have not sinned only because we were not tempted. Softly—we whom *pride*, not *principle*, has saved. Softly—we whose lives the world writes fair, and perhaps God's eye leprously foul.

COUNTRY MATINS.—He who sleeps at early dawn in the country, stops his ears to the prayers of Nature. That early tuneful waking! What can compare with it? Evening is soothing and sweet, with its stars and its calm; but the gradual brightness of the new day, softly stealing upon us, as the tints deepen and the songs strengthen, till the full orchestra is complete, oh! this is soul strengthening and sublime! We were weak of purpose, we were dispirited, the night before. Yesterday had overlapped its cares, and our tired shoulders shrank from the coming burden. But this bright resurrection heralded so thrillingly by soulless creatures! Shall *we* immortals only be thankless and dumb? We join the chorus! Care sits lightly at this blessed hour. All things for that day are possible to us—hard duty sweet. Blessed be God, then, for the sweet dawning of each new day!

A TRIP TO THE CAATSKILLS.

WELL—I've "done" the Caatskills! I've tugged up that steep mountain, one of the hottest days in which a quadruped or a biped ever perspired, packed to suffocation, with other gasping sufferers, in that crucifying institution called a stage-coach, until I became resignedly indifferent, whether it reached its destination, or rolled head over heels—or rather head over wheels —over the precipice. Landing at last at the hotel, I was conscious of only one want—a bedroom; which, when obtained, was close enough, and which I shared with three other jaded mortals. The next morning, thanks to a good Providence and the landlord, I emigrated into unexceptionable quarters.

Ah—now I breathe! now I remember no more that purgatorial reeling stage-coach, and its protracted jigglings—wrigglings—joltings and bumpings. Now I am repaid—now I gaze—oh, how *can* I gaze with only one pair of eyes, on all this beauty and magnificence? This vast plain spread out so far below our feet like an immense garden, with its luxuriant foliage—its little cottages, smaller than a child's toy: its noble river, specked with white sails, lessened by distance to a silver thread, winding through the meadows; and beyond—still other plains, other streams, other mountains—on—on—stretching far beyond the dizzy ken, till the eye fills, and the heart swells, and leaning in an ecstasy of happiness on the bosom of "Our Father," we cry, "Oh! what is man that Thou art mindful of him?"

Now—as if the scene were too gorgeous for mortal sight, nature gently, compassionately drops a silvery veil of mist before it, veiling, yet not hiding—withdrawing, yet not removing—giving us now sunshine, now shadow; bringing out now the vivid green of a meadow, now the silver sheen of the river; now the bold outline of a pine-girdled mountain. And now—the scene changes, and fleets of clouds sail slowly—glide ghostly, round the mountain's base; winding-sheets wrapped round the shapely trees, from which they burst with a glorious resurrection; while over and above all arches the blue heavens, smiling that it canopies a scene so fair. See—village after village, like specks in the distance—where human hearts throb to human joys and sorrows; where restless ambition flutters against the barred cage of necessity, pining for the mountain-top of freedom; when, gained, oh, weary traveller, to lose its distant golden splendor, and wrap thee in the chill vapors of discontent. What matter—if thou but accept this proof of thy immortality? Yes—village after village; farmers plodding on, as farmers too often will, turning up the soil for dollars and cents, seeing only in the clouds the filter for their crops; in the lakes the refrigerator for their fish; in the glorious trees their fuel; in the waving grass and sloping meadows, feed for their cattle; in the sweet sunrise an alarm bell to labor, in the little bird's vespers but a call to feed and sleep.

Now—twilight steals upon the mountains, calm as heaven. The bright valleys sleep in their deepening shadows, while on the mountain-tops lingers the glory, as if loath to fade into the perfumed night. With a graceful sweep the little bird mounts to the clouds, takes his last circling flight, and sings his evening hymn, sweet and soft as the rapt soul's whispered farewell to earth. And yet— O God!—this is but the porch to the temple, before whose dazzling splendors even Thy seraphs veil their sinless eyes.

In an article in a late weekly, I was shocked at a flippant and unfeeling allusion to "the yellow invalids one meets at watering-places." Surely, the sight of such, wandering forth with feeble step and faded eyes, taking their last look at this beautiful earth, side by side with the rosy cheek and bounding pulse of health, should excite in us only feelings of tenderest love and compassion. Some such I met; but I would not, if I could, that their pale faces should have been banished from our merry circle. It was no damper on my enjoyment to gaze at their drooping eyelids, and listlessly crossed hands. I would but have yielded them the cosiest corner on the sofa, or the most comfortable arm-chair, or the sunniest nook on the piazza, or tempted their failing appetite with the daintiest bit at the table. I would like to have taken their transparent hands in my healthy palm, and given them a kindly grasp, by which they would recognize me in that better land, which every day dawns clearer on my sight. It is well that we should have such in our midst; and surely none whose hearts are drawn by yearning, but invisible cords, to the dear ones who *once* made sunlight in our homes, can fail to recognize and respond to the tacit claims of the stranger-invalid upon our tenderest sympathies.

And while upon this subject, I would speak a word, which, it seems to me, needs to be spoken—upon a courteous recognition of the lonely, unobtrusive traveller, who, for the time, makes one of the same family under a hotel roof. It is easy for all to pay court to the distinguished, the handsome, or the agreeable; to seek an introduction to such, or manufacture a pretext for speaking. It is for the unattractive I would plead, and the aged—for those who have nothing to recommend them to notice, save that they are unnoticed. It seems to me that one need study no book of etiquette to find out, that a passing salutation to such, a kind inquiry after their health, an offer of a flower—when one has been rambling where their weary feet may not go—is the true politeness. One feels like spurning the civility received at the hands of those who see not in these disregarded ones the lineaments of the same Father. It gives me pleasure to say that

I have witnessed some noble examples of courtesy to such, extended with a graceful ease, which would seem less to confer a favor than to receive one by their acceptance.

It was very pleasant to see little children at the Caatskills; but they were all too few. Children are generally supposed to be bad travellers: this is a mistake. They have often more self-denial, fortitude, and endurance than half your grown people. I can answer at least for one little girl under my charge from whom no amount of burning sun, hunger, or fatigue, extorted a syllable of complaint; in fact, I once saw her endure a car collision with the same commendable philosophy, while men old enough to be her father were frantic with affright. "Render unto children their due," is on the fly-leaf of *my* Bible.

Yes, it is good for them to go out of cities. A city child is a cruel, wicked, shapeless, one-sided abortion. 'Tis a pale shoot of a plant, struggling bravely for its little day of life in some rayless corner, all unblest by the warm sunshine which God intended to give to it color, strength, and fragrance. What wonder that the blight falls on it? Do you say, Pshaw? Do you suppose a child, for instance, could appreciate the scenery at the Caatskills? I ask you, do all the *adults* who flock there to gaze, appreciate it? Do you not hear the words "divine," —"enchanting,"—"beautiful,"—"magnificent,"— applied by them, as often to costume as to clouds? Give me a child's appreciation of such a scene, before that of two-thirds of the adult gazers. Its thought may be half-fledged, and given with lisping utterance, but it *is* a thought. The eyes, while speaking, may suddenly change their look of wondering awe, for one of elfish fun; what matter! The feeling was sincere, though fleeting—genuine, though fragmentary. By and by that little child, leaving its sports, will come back again to my side as I sit upon the rocks; and any gray-haired philosopher who can, may answer the question with which she seals my lips; any poet who can, may coin a phrase which, more fitly than her's, symbols nature's beauty. Now she's off to play again—leaving the deep question unanswered, but not for that reason to be forgotten—no more than the rock, or mountain, or river, which called it forth, and which is hung up like a cabinet picture in that childish memory, to be clouded over, it may be, by the dust and discolorations of after years, but never destroyed—waiting quietly that master touch, which obliterating all else, as if trivial or unworthy, restores only to the fading eye of age, in freshened beauty, the glowing pictures of childhood.

The great charm of the Caatskills is its constant variety; look where you may, you shall never see twice the same effect of light and shade. Again, and again I said to myself, How, amid such prodigal, changeful beauty, shall the artist choose? Life were all too short for the decision. Ever the busy finger of Omnipotence, silently showing us wonder upon wonder. "Silently," did I say? Ah, no; ever writing, on cloud and valley, rock, mountain, and river—"all these as a scroll shall be rolled away, but My Word shall never pass away."

I have not spoken of the lovely rides in the vicinity of the Caatskills, of which we were not slow to avail ourselves. Turn which way we would, all was beauty. And yet, not all—I must not forget among these magnificent mountains the hateful, bare, desolate, treeless, vineless, old-fashioned schoolhouse, resembling a covered pound for stray calves. What a sight it was, to be sure, to see the weary children swarm out into the warm sunshine, shouting for very joy that they *might* shout, and trying their poor cramped limbs to see if they had not actually lost the use of them in those inquisitorially devised seats. Alas! what an alphabet might a teacher who was a *child-lover* have deciphered, *outside* those purgatorial walls, on trees, and flowers, and mountains; the teaching of which would have needed no quickening ferule, cramped no restless limbs, overtasked and diseased no forming brain! What streams of knowledge, waiting only the divining rod of the lover of God, and His representatives—*little children*—to freshen and to beautify wheresoever they should flow!

Yes—it was good to see those children kicking their reprieved heels in the air—I only wish they could have kicked over that desolate old schoolhouse. *They* didn't know why I nodded to them such a merry good day; they never will know, poor victims, how royally well I sympathized with their somersets on the grass—they thought, perhaps, that I knew the "school-marm;"—Heaven forbid—I would rather know the incendiary who should set fire to her school-house!

In one neighborhood—which is so small that an undertaker must be sorely puzzled to find subjects—I noticed a hideous picture of a coffin stuck on the front of a small dwelling-house, with a repulsive ostentation that outdid even New York. This, to an invalid visiting the Caatskills for health (and there are many such), must be an inspiriting sight!

This summer travel, after all, is a most excellent thing. It is well for people from different parts of the country to rub off their local angles by collision. It is well for those of opposite temperaments and habits of thought, to look each other mentally in the face. It is well for the indefatigable mother and housekeeper to remain ignorant, for one blessed month, of the inevitable, "What shall we have for dinner?" It is well for the man of business, whose thoughts are narrowed down to stocks and stores, to look out on the broad hills, and let the little bird's song stir memories of days when heaven was nearer to him than it has ever been since. It is well for the ossified old bachelor to air his selfishness in the genial atmosphere of woman's smile. It is well for the overtasked clergyman, and his equally overtasked (though not equally salaried) wife, to have a brief breathing spell from vestries and verjuice. It is well for their daughter, who has been tied up to the parish pillory of—" you must not do this," and "you must not do that," and "you must not do the other," till she begins to think that God did not know what He was about when He made her, to bestow so many powers, and tastes, and faculties, which must be forever folded up in a napkin, for fear of offending "Mrs. Grundy." *It is well for the Editor, that he may look in the faces of the women whose books he has reviewed, and condemned, too, without reading a blessed word of them.* It is well for everybody —even the exclusives who hesitate, through fear of plebeian contamination, to sit down in the common parlor; because, were all the world wise—which Heaven forbid—there would be nothing to laugh at!

A lack of competition is said to affect progress. That the traveller to the Caatskills has no choice but "The Mountain House," should not, it seems to me, act as an extinguisher to enterprise upon its well-patronized landlord. I might make many suggestions as to improvements, by which I am sure he would, in the end, be no loser. It needs no great stretch of the imagination to fancy the carriage which conveys victims to "The Falls," a relic of the Inquisition. I did not know till I had tried it, how many evolutions a comfortably-fleshed woman could perform in a minute, between the roof and floor of such a ve-higgle! (Result—a villanous headache— and the black and blues.) I noticed a small bookshelf in the very pleasant ladies' parlor. "Praise God Barebones," I think, must have made the selection of the volumes. But it is pleasanter to commend than to find fault. I could forgive many shortcomings for the privilege of feasting on the wholesome light bread, which to a saleratus-consuming—saleratus-consumed New Yorker, was glory enough to nibble at. Blessings, too, on the skilful fingers which stirred up those appetizing omelettes and sublime orange-puddings. What an amusement it is, to be sure, to watch a man when he gets hold of the dish he fancies! What fun to bother him with innumerable questions while he is trying to eat it in undisturbed rapture—meanwhile wishing you at the North Pole! How cynical the creatures are, the last interminable half hour *before* meals, and how sweetly amiable and lazy *after!* Then is your time to try men's soles; to insist upon their taking a walk with you, when they can scarce waddle; when visions of curling Havana smoke invite them to two-legged piazza-chairs, digestion, and meditation. *Then* is your time to be suddenly seized with an unpostponable longing for a brisk game of ten-pins, to test the sincerity of all their disinterested speeches. My dears, the man who continues amiable while you thus stroke his inclinations the wrong way, may safely be trusted in any matrimonial crisis. I indorse him.

With regard to the Falls it may be a delusion, but I think it is rather a damper to sentiment to fee a man to turn on the water for them! and I know it is a damper to the slippers to go down into the ravine beneath—which, joking aside, is very beautiful, and a great place for a bear to hug you in. Instead of which, I met a young parson whom I knew by token of his very black coat, and very white necktie; and who actually pulled from his sacerdotal pocket a profane handkerchief which I had carelessly dropped, presenting it with as much gravity as if he had been giving me "the right hand of fellowship." Heaven help him—so young—so well-made—and so solemn!—I felt immensely like a frolic. And speaking of frolics—oh, the mountains I had to leave unclimbed, the "campings out" foregone—and all because I was forcordained to petticoats—hampering, bush-catching petticoats!—all because I hadn't courage to put on trousers (in which, by the way, I have made several unsatisfactory private rehearsal attempts to unsex myself, but nature was too much for me), and wade knee-deep in moss to see what man alone, by privilege of his untrammelled apparel, may feast his eyes upon. It is a *crying* shame. Ten-pins, too; who can get a "ten-strike" in petticoats? See what I would do at it in a jacket and unmentionables, though I really think nature had no eye to this game when she modelled a woman's hand and wrist. Now I dare say there are straight-laced people who will be shocked at the idea of a woman playing ten-pins. Well, let them be shocked. I vote for it for two reasons; first, for the exercise, when dripping grass and lowering skies deny it to us elsewhere; secondly, because it is always a pleasant sight to see husbands sharing this, or any other innocent recreation, with their wives and daughters, instead of herding selfishly in male flocks. I like this feature of domesticity in pleasure-seeking in our friends, the Germans. I like the Germans. Their joy is infectious. A sprinkling of such spirits would do much towards infusing a little life into the solemn business way in which Americans too often pursue, but seldom overtake, pleasure. Yes, it is a lovely sight to see them with their families! and oh, how much more honorable and just, to a painstaking, economical wife and mother, than the expensive meal, shared at a restaurant with some male companion, while she sits solitary, to whom a proposal even for a simple walk would be happiness, as an evidence of that watchful care which is so endearing to a wife's heart.

Not the least among our enjoyments were our evenings at the Caatskills. When warm enough, promenading on the ample piazza with pleasant friends; when the out-door temperature forbade this, seated in the parlors, listening to merry voices, looking on young and happy faces, or, what is never less beautiful, upon those who, having reached life's summit, did not, for that reason, churlishly refuse to cast back approving, sympathizing glances upon the young loiterers who were still gleefully gathering flowers by the way.

Then, too, we had music, *heart* music, from our German friend; whose artistic fingers often, also, gave harmonious expressions upon the piano to our *sunrise* thoughts, before we had left our rooms. Happy they, whose full souls can lighten their secret burdens by the low musical plaint, understood only by those who have themselves loved and suffered!

Of how many tried and aching hearts has music been the eloquent voice? The ruffled brow grows smooth beneath its influence; the angry feeling, calm as a wayward child, at a mother's loving kiss. Joy, like a white-robed angel, glides softly in, and on the billows of earthly sorrow she lays her gentle finger, whispering, "Peace, be still!"

A SHAM EXPOSED.—A great deal is said about young men "who are not able to marry on account of the extravagance of women," when these very young men often spend as much on their own superfluities, if not on their vices, as would support a *reasonable* wife. But the laugh comes in here—that such young men don't *really* want a *reasonable* wife! They pass by the industrious, self-denying young girl, who pluckily resolves not to let an already overtasked father or brother support her, and pay court to some be-flounced and be-jewelled pink-and-white doll, and then whine that they "can't get married to her, because she is so extravagant." That's the whole truth about it; and when young men face and acknowledge it in a manly manner, it will be soon enough to listen to them on the "marriage" question.

THE TRIP TO BROMPTON.

"WHAT a splendid day to go to Brompton!" exclaimed Mr. Smith, looking out of the open window and breathing in the fresh air as only a man can who has been pent up in a counting-room till his head feels as though it had a full-sized windmill going inside. "Come, wife, pick up your traps, and let's be off; the train starts in an hour, and there is a return-train at nine this evening; just the time to come back." Mrs. Smith looked lovingly at her baby, for weary as she was, it was a trial to leave it behind. Who knew what perfidious pin might torture it, or how hard it might sneeze without even a sympathizing "coo" to reassure its startled timidity. Who knew but its milk might choke it, or a window be left open that should be shut; or shut that should be opened. Who knew but some passing fish-horn, or shad distributor, might scare it into fits, with unearthly and prolonged whooping. Who knew that it might not pull the sheet over its face in its sleep and smother itself, or be laid too near the edge of the bed, and roll off. In short, come to think of it, Mrs. Smith felt that she had better stay and attend to these little matters. But an executive hand thrust her bonnet on her head, and parasol in hand, she found herself on the way to the depot.

It *was* pleasant, after one *did* finally emerge from that smothering depot. The smell of fresh earth and fresh-springing grass, and the birds' song, and the vivid green of the trees, were all delicious. Mrs. Smith felt as if she had but half existed for months, something as a buried toad might, who had lain all winter under a big cold stone, and crept out some fine morning to try his hopping powers in the June sunshine. She took no heed of the oranges "five for a shill*in*" thrust in her face, nor of that dreariest of all things, "a comic newspaper;" nor packages of "refined candies," or "fig paste," or "Indian moccasins," or any of the modern inventions to disturb the serenity of quiet, reflective travellers. She looked steadily out of the window at the glimpses of wood, and water, and blue sky to be seen therefrom; nor noticed the flirtation on a side-seat between a young school-girl and her juvenile beau; nor the fine bonnet that a lady in front thought it good taste to be travelling in. It was all one to her, while that sweet, soft wind soothed her heated temples, and she was borne along without any effort of her own so deliciously. But all pleasures must have an end, more's the pity; so had this. "Brompton Station," bawled the conductor, breaking the spell; and with a conjugal reminding nudge of Mr. Smith's elbow, Mrs. Smith found her feet, and alighted. "It was just a mile," so the depot-master said, to the house where they were looking for "Summer board." "*Only* a mile—let's walk, then," said Mrs. Smith; "what a nice road, and what big trees; and how sweet the air is." But alas! Mrs. Smith was mortal, and she had before starting disdained dinner. Her exclamations of delight began to grow fainter as they proceeded, and in half an hour, a seat on the top of a stone wall was a consummation devoutly to be wished. Perched there, with dangling gaiter-boots, Mrs. Smith faintly inquired of a cow-boy, "how far to Brompton?" "A mile, *mum*." "But they told us *that* at the station, and we've *been* a mile," she gasped. "It's a good piece yet," he replied, with a scratch of the head. "Do you think that man yonder would take me up in his cart?" whispered Mrs. Smith confidentially to her husband. "Perhaps so," he replied; "but there's no seat in it, and you'd be horribly jolted." "So I should—dear me—I shall know what 'a mile' is, next time," replied Mrs. Smith, as she rolled like a bag of wool from the fence to the ground, and settling her bonnet, started again on her travels. "Isn't that a splendid view, May?" asked Mr. Smith. "I suppose so," replied his wife. "Oh, John, I'm awful hungry; and I cannot go any farther; and I *won't*," said she, sitting down on a big, flat stone. People don't always know what they will do; as Mrs. Smith said this she sprang to her feet, and went down the road with the velocity of a steam-engine. The innocent cow, who was the unconscious propelling cause, looked as much astonished as Mr. Smith; but it is an ill wind that blows nobody good, and the farm-house, thanks to that cow, was finally reached. A cup of tea, and some "domestic bread," set all right with Mrs. Smith. What was "a mile" now? She climbed fences, just as if she had no baby at home; she pulled roses, and lilacs, and grasses, and peeped into pig-sties, and ferreted little kittens out of the barn, and, in short, one would scarcely have recognized her as the forlorn lady in the dangling gaiter-boots perched on a wayside wall. And so the afternoon wore away, and thoughts of "baby" began to clamor. Just then appeared Mr. Smith, with a serious face. "What is it?" asked his wife, with that conjugal free-masonry which beats "Lodges" all hollow. "There's no train back to-night. May, I made a mistake, and read the time-table wrong; I'm sorry; but it was nine $A. M.$, instead of nine $P. M.$; so we shall have to stay till morning." "John," said Mrs. Smith, solemnly, "is there a freight train that goes down any time during the night?" "I don't know; I can ask," said her husband; "but you can't go on a freight-train—it is so high, that you can't step in or out, even if the conductor will take you; and then there will be cattle aboard, perhaps, and you'll be cooped in a close, little pen, full of tobacco-smoke;—just think! *tobacco-smoke!*" said Mr. Smith. "You know you never can stand *that*, May." "Just ask if that cattle-train is *really* going, and *when*," replied his wife, with a far-off look in her eyes, as if she could see her wailing baby in the distance. "Well, it may go at one at night, and it may go at two; it stops to take in milk for the city at the different stations, and it is often an hour behind time."

An hour after this conversation, Mrs. Smith found herself reclining on the sofa, in the parlor of the small country tavern, opposite the depot, which latter was closed for the night, waiting the arrival of the "cattle-train," while Mr. Smith consoled himself with a cigar on the piazza. She was roused from a light nap by a tap on the window; a marital nose was flattened against the window-pane, through which the information was conveyed her that *she* was locked *in* for the night and *he* was locked out.

Mrs. Smith flattened *her* nose against the window-pane and inquired, "What was to be done?" "Open the window, of course." "I can't—I don't understand it. I can't see how it goes. The thing is nailed down. It won't stir an inch." "Pshaw! press your finger on that little knob, you goose." And the goose did it; and directly a pair of gaiter-boots were seen going through the window. That was nice; but the chill river-fog soon began to penetrate cloak and dress, and slight shivers ensued: and the bouquet of roses and lilacs was thrown away in disgust, for both hands were needed to fold her drapery more closely round. The sad-voiced "whip-poor-will" began his midnight serenade; and puffing bull-frogs joined in the chorus, and watch-dogs barked, and little chickens peeped, and roosters mistook the moonlight for broad day, and gave shrill, premature crows—and still the cattle-train came not; and Mrs. Smith sat crouched on a wheelbarrow-looking affair, used for trundling trunks at the depot, thinking of "baby." Whoo—puff—puff—whoo! "There it is; ask no questions, May, but run ahead, and get in somehow." It *was* "somehow." May never knew how—for John and the conductor managed it between them, much to the detriment of skirts and frills, and May found herself in company with a kerosene lamp and a greasy cushion; and through the partition friendly cows were greeting her; and the air was odorous with tobacco-smoke; and the cars bumped and jolted and thumped as if they were bewitched; and there was nothing to hold on to, or to lean against; and sometimes her bonnet touched the wall, and sometimes unexpectedly, she had no chair under her; and so, at two in the morning, this pleasure-seeking couple were landed about three miles from their city residence, and *not* in the vicinity of a livery stable, and caught by mere good luck an infrequent street car ; and, reaching home, counted the baby's toes and fingers and found them all right; and over their early coffee laughed at the " trip to Brompton."

LAKE GEORGE REVISITED.

LAKE GEORGE has haunted me since I saw it. I thought to abide at peace in mine easy-chair this summer, but Lake George was not visible from my windows; and how could I let the summer days shine on its beauty and I not by to see? and then that glorious Hudson! for a sight of which I am *always* longing. There was no help for it; I went through the packing purgatory, and set sail. Commend me to steamboat travel over and above all the cars that ever screeched under and above ground; but, alas! steamboats have a drawback which cars have not. You get a comfortable seat on deck, on the shady side; in a chair *with a back* to it. You say this is pleasant, as you fold your hands—Ugh! So does a man, or a group of them near you, who have just lighted their cigars, or worse, their pipes. Puff—puff—puff; straight into your face; right and left; fore and aft. Is this the " fresh air " for which you were travelling? You reluctantly change your place. You even take a seat in the sun, to rid yourself of the smoke. Puff —puff; another smoker sits, or stands, near you; you turn disgusted away, only to encounter another group, who evidently regard the beautiful Hudson only in the light of an enormous spittoon.

Now I protest against this lack of decency and chivalry. If no other woman dare brave these gentlemen, (?) I will, though I know well what anathemas I shall incur. I call, moreover, upon all *decent* steamboat-captains to provide a den for these tobacco-absorbing, tobacco-emitting gentry, in some part of the boat where women are *not*. If they must smoke, which point I neither deny nor admit, do not suffer them to expel ladies, to whom they are so profuse in——fine speeches—to the stifling air of the ladies' cabin, to avoid it. This at least seems but reasonable and fair. The only place where one is really in no danger of this nuisance at present is in church; though I am expecting every Sunday to see boots on the tops of pews, and lighted cigars behind them. Oh, I know very well that some ladies *pretend* to "like it," because they had rather endure it than resign the attentions of a gentleman who don't know any better than to ask them "if it is disagreeable." *Of course*, it is disagreeable, for women are clean creatures; and if they tell you it is *not*, know that they tell you a good-natured but most unmitigated fib; and you should be ashamed of availing yourself of it to make yourselves such nuisances.

That lovely midnight glide up the Hudson! Lying dreamly on one's pillow; just asleep enough to know nothing disagreeable, and awake enough to see with half-closed eyes through your little window the white sails, and green shores, and listen to the plashing water. Daylight and Albany, with its noisy pier, seem an impertinence. "Breakfast?" ah, yes—we are human, and love coffee; but the melancholy figures and faces, as we emerge from our stateroom! Rosy mouths agape; bright eyes half-veiled with heavy lids; cloaks and mantles tossed on with more haste than taste; hair tumbled, bonnets awry. Pull down your veils, ladies, and prepare yourselves for a general dislocation of every bone in your body, as you thunder up to the hotel in *that* omnibus, which is bound back again in exactly three seconds, for another hapless cargo.

Your "unprotected female" is to be met everywhere. Is my countenance so benevolent that she should have singled me out, as I waited at the hotel for my breakfast? There she was—with spectacles on nose, carpet-bag in hand; alert—nervous—distracted.

"Was I travelling North or South?"

Was it for want of coffee, or geography, that I curtly replied: "I haven't the least idea, Ma'am."

"Was I alone, dear?"

"Husband, Ma'am."

"Where's the —— House, dear?"

"*This* is it, Ma'am."

"Lord bless me—I thought it was the Depot!"

There may be individuals existing who have not ridden in *that* stage-coach from "Moreau Station" to Lake George. If so, let him or her, particularly *her*, bear in mind, in selecting her attitude on sitting down, that it is final and irrevocable, spite of cramps, for thirteen good miles of sunny, sandy, up-and-down-hill, bumping, thumping travel. However, there's fun even in that. Jolts bring out jokes. After punching daylight through the ribs of one's neighbor, one don't wait for an "introduction." Your Cologne bottle becomes common property, also your fan. If there is an unlucky wight on top, whose overhanging boots betoken a due respect for the eighth commandment, of course he can have the refusal of your sun umbrella to keep his brains from frying, particularly as you don't know what to do with it inside. Yes—on the whole, it is fun; but it isn't fun to arrive at a hotel faint, dusty, hungry, and hear, "We are running over, but we can *feed* you here, if you'll *lodge* in the village." May do for men, groan out the green veils; try at another house. Ah, now it is *our* turn; installed by some hocus-pocus in two rooms commanding a magnificent view of the lake, we can afford to pity hungry wretches who can't get in. Now we breathe! Our feet and arms—yes, they are all right, for we just tried them. Now we toss off our bonnet, and gaze at those huge mountains and their dark shadows on the lake; now we see the little row-boats glide along, to the musical, sparkling dip of the oar; now we hear the merry laughs of the rowers, or perhaps a snatch of a song in a woman's voice. Now the clear, fresh breeze sweeps over the hills, and ruffles the lake, bringing us spicy odors. Oh, but this is delicious. Dress? What, *here?* No, indeed; enough of that in New

York. Who wants to see dresses may look in our trunks. That hill is to be climbed, that shore to be reached, that boat to be sailed in, and how is that to be done if one " dresses " ? We are for a tramp, a sail, a drive—anything but dressing.

Lake George by moonlight, at midnight! oh, you should see it, with its shining, quivering path of light, as if for angel footsteps. I know not whether another world is fairer than this; but I *do* know that *there* are no sighs, no weary outstretching of the hands for help, no smothered cry of despair.

SELF-HELP.—We pity those who do not and never have "labored." *Ennui* and satiety sooner or later are sure to be their portion. Like the child who is in possession of every new toy, and who has snapped and broken them all, they stand looking about for something—*anything* new and amusing; and like this child, they often stoop to the mud and the gutter for it. It is an understood principle of human nature, that people never value that which is easily obtained. Bread which has been purchased with unearned money has never the flavor and sweetness of that which is won by the sweat of one's own brow.

COOKERY AND TAILORING.

WHEN male writers have nothing else to say they fall "afoul" of all women for not being adepts in cookery. Now, one might just as well insist that every man should know how to make his own trousers, as that every woman should be a cook.

Suppose reverses should come, and the man who don't know how should not be able to employ a tailor, where would he be then, not understanding how to make his own trousers? And suppose reverses should *not* come, how much wiser and better for him to know practically all about tailoring, so that he might *with knowledge* be able to direct his tailor? At present he thoughtlessly steps in and recklessly orders them. How does he know whether the amount of cloth used is necessary, or the contrary? How does he know that he isn't swindled fearfully on buttons, lappets, and facings, and even the padding inserted to make his rickety figure bewitching? I grieve when I think of this, and then of his asking his wife afterward, "what she did with the twenty-five cents he gave her yesterday to go shopping with." He ought to be master of tailoring in all its branches, before he links his destiny with a woman, or else he ought to wear a cloak, which, morally speaking, *is* his normal condition.

He may reply that he don't like tailoring; that he has no gift for tailoring; that studying it ever so long he should only make a bad tailor, to spoil the making of a good lawyer or doctor. That's nothing to the purpose. I insist that he shall learn *tailoring;* not only that, but I insist that he shall *like* it too. His lawyering and doctoring can come in afterward wheresoever the gods will, in the chinks of his time, but breeches and coats he shall know how to make, or every editor in the land shall be down on him whenever they are hard up for an editorial, if, without this important branch of knowledge, he presumes to address a political meeting. For not understanding breeches, how the mischief can he understand politics, or be prepared to speak about them?

He may tell me that he don't intend to "link his destiny with woman," but instead, to be a gay bachelor, and have a latch-key, and one towel a week at some boarding-house, and whistle "Hail Columbia" at midnight, at his own sweet will, with variations, without the fear of waking some wretched baby. *That's* nothing to do with it. I insist that even *then*, he, being obliged to wear breeches, should know how many yards of different width cloth it takes to make them. I insist that, without this knowledge, he is not even prepared to be a bachelor. Nobody can tell, in this world, when misfortune may overtake one. Cigars may become so dear, and his exchequer so low in consequence, that he may be obliged to alter his little plan, and link his destiny to some woman who will earn them for him. And suppose the twins should afterward interfere with her earnings, then think how glorious it would be to turn his knowledge of tailoring to account on this conjugal rainy day, and not only make his own breeches, but those of the twins, who would undoubtedly be boys, because men like boys, and therefore ought to have them.

Now, having freed my mind on this point, I proceed to say that the brightest and most gifted women I have known have perfectly understood cookery, and have written some of their best things over the cooking-stove, while they kept *two* " pots boiling." Furthermore, that the more brains a woman has, the less she will " look down upon," or " despise," a knowledge so important as that of cookery. But because she knows how, and because she does it, it need not of necessity follow that she " hankers after it." And *when* she does it, she should have the credit of doing it; and if her husband be a literary man, he should know and acknowledge— which is the thing he don't always do—that though she resolutely performs her duty without shirking, while he quietly scribbles, a sigh occasionally goes up chimney with the smoke, at the thoughts which fly up with it, that she may never catch again, either for fame or money. I say, when gobbling down the food she prepares, or oversees the preparing, in these days of incompetent servants, he should sometimes recognize this.

Then I would call attention to the fact that married men should everywhere, and in all classes, remember, that it is very discouraging for any wife and housekeeper, when, for the same efficient labor which she expends under her own roof, she could earn for herself at least a competence, to be obliged to go as a *beggar* to her husband for the money which is justly her *due*. Perhaps, if husbands were more just and generous with regard to this matter, women might take their pleasure in "cookery," which every man seems to think is her only "through ticket" to Paradise, and to their affections, *viâ* their stomachs.

TAKE A VACATION.—It need not of necessity be an expensive one. Go away, if only for a week, and shake off the drudgery of routine. Some people are of the opinion that upon their return they will find work all the more difficult. It is not so. The vacation judiciously spent, and according to one's means, will give increased strength for the performance of the duties awaiting us. Let those who cannot do this, take now and then a car-ride into the country, for a day of fresh air. A sight of the green grass and clover-blossoms will do them good. Continuous, unremitting labor is not good either for man or beast.

UP THE HUDSON.

I SUPPOSE nobody is to blame, but I feel indignant every time I take a steamboat sail up the Hudson, that I was not born a New Yorker. I am not particularly fond of sleeping on a shelf, or eating bread and butter in that submarine *Tophet*, called the "Dining Cabin;" were it not for these little drawbacks, I think I should engage board for a month on one of our Hudson river steamboats (one that *doesn't* patronize "Calliopes").

As to a "residence on the banks of the Hudson," do you think I would so sacrilegiously and audaciously familiarize myself with its glorious beauty? I decline on the principle that the lover, who had pleasurably wooed for years, refused to marry, "because he should have nowhere to spend his evenings;" where, oh, where, *I* ask, should I spend my *summers?* Yes, a month's board on a Hudson river steamboat! *a floating boarding-house!* why not? I claim the idea as original. First stipulation— meals and mattresses *on deck*, in fair weather.

What a curious study are travellers! How the human nature comes out! There are your men and women, bound to get their money's worth, to the last dime, and who imagine that bullying and bluster is the way, not only to do this, but to deceive people into the belief that they are accustomed to being waited upon at home. Of such are the men who wander ceaselessly upstairs and downstairs and in my ladies' cabin, smoking and yawning, poking their walking-sticks into every bundle and basket from sheer ennui,—and ever and anon returning on deck, suspiciously wiping their mouths. Of such are they who light a pipe or cigar in the immediate proximity of ladies, who have just secured a comfortable seat on deck, that they may revel in the much-longed-for fresh sea-breeze; dogged, obstinate, "deil take the hindmost," selfish, ruffianly cubs, who would stand up on their hind legs in a twinkling at the insinuation that they were not ".gentlemen."

Yes, there are all sorts on board a steamboat; there is your country-woman in her best toggery; fancy bonnet, brass ear-rings, and the inevitable "locket;" who, when the gong sounds, takes out a huge basket to dine off molasses-cake, drop-cake, doughnuts, and cheese; who coolly nudges some man in the ribs "to lend her the loan" of his jack-knife, wherewith she dexterously cuts up and harpoons into a mouth more useful than ornamental, little square blocks of "soggy" gingerbread, with a trusting confidence in the previous habits of that strange jack-knife, that is delicious to witness! Then there are quicksilver little children, frightening mothers into fits, by peering into dangerous places, and leaning over the deck into the water;

UP THE HUDSON.

I SUPPOSE nobody is to blame, but I feel indignant every time I take a steamboat sail up the Hudson, that I was not born a New Yorker. I am not particularly fond of sleeping on a shelf, or eating bread and butter in that submarine *Tophet*, called the "Dining Cabin;" were it not for these little drawbacks, I think I should engage board for a month on one of our Hudson river steamboats (one that *doesn't* patronize "Calliopes").

As to a "residence on the banks of the Hudson," do you think I would so sacrilegiously and audaciously familiarize myself with its glorious beauty? I decline on the principle that the lover, who had pleasurably wooed for years, refused to marry, "because he should have nowhere to spend his evenings;" where, oh, where, *I* ask, should I spend my *summers?* Yes, a month's board on a Hudson river steamboat! *a floating boarding-house!* why not? I claim the idea as original. First stipulation—meals and mattresses *on deck*, in fair weather.

What a curious study are travellers! How the human nature comes out! There are your men and women, bound to get their money's worth, to the last dime, and who imagine that bullying and bluster is the way, not only to do this, but to deceive people into the belief that they are accustomed to being waited upon at home. Of such are the men who wander ceaselessly upstairs and downstairs and in my ladies' cabin, smoking and yawning, poking their walking-sticks into every bundle and basket from sheer ennui,—and ever and anon returning on deck, suspiciously wiping their mouths. Of such are they who light a pipe or cigar in the immediate proximity of ladies, who have just secured a comfortable seat on deck, that they may revel in the much-longed-for fresh sea-breeze; dogged, obstinate, "deil take the hindmost," selfish, ruffianly cubs, who would stand up on their hind legs in a twinkling at the insinuation that they were not "gentlemen."

Yes, there are all sorts on board a steamboat; there is your country-woman in her best toggery; fancy bonnet, brass ear-rings, and the inevitable "locket;" who, when the gong sounds, takes out a huge basket to dine off molasses-cake, drop-cake, doughnuts, and cheese; who coolly nudges some man in the ribs "to lend her the loan" of his jack-knife, wherewith she dexterously cuts up and harpoons into a mouth more useful than ornamental, little square blocks of "soggy" gingerbread, with a trusting confidence in the previous habits of that strange jack-knife, that is delicious to witness! Then there are quicksilver little children, frightening mothers into fits, by peering into dangerous places, and leaning over the deck into the water;

fresh air; and that is a luxury that is always denied to lecturers. They'll applaud him, and they'll ask him "what he'll drink," and they'll take him to execution in a carriage, and take his corpse back in a carriage, but they won't let him breathe, at least till they've done with him, and I shouldn't long survive such politeness. Then the stereotyped pitcher of water would close my lips instead of helping to open them. I hate a pitcher of water. I got a boxed ear for saying that once; but I've got two ears, that's a comfort, so I'll say it again. Then, I couldn't lecture because I should feel cold shivers down my back, when that awful chairman rose and said, "Ladies and gentlemen, allow me to introduce to you the speaker for this evening, FANNY FERN." I hate that. I should want to hop up and speak when I got ready—say—while the lovers in the audience were whispering to each other, and the old ladies settling where to put their "umberils," and the old gentlemen hunting their pockets for their "spettacles" which they had left at home, and the old maids trying to find a seat where "a horrid man" wasn't too near. I'd like to pounce on them, like a cat, just then, and give my first scratch and draw blood; and then they'd let me go on my own way; because, you see, I am one of those persons who can't do anything "to order." I often see in the papers advertisements of "shirts made—to order," but I never yet saw an advertisement of a corresponding female garment made that way. Did you? Well, that's a hint that females shouldn't be hampered by stupid rules and precedents. But this is a digression.

Again, I couldn't lecture because I can't bear saleratus, and I suppose all my engagements wouldn't be in cities. Then, nextly, I couldn't lecture, because, after the lecture was over, I should be "dead beat;" and that is just the time everybody would hurry into the committee-room to tell me that I was; and to use a dozen dictionaries, to advise "me not to talk," but to go right straight home and go to bed as soon—as *they* had got through talking with me!

Lastly, the reason I can't lecture is because I am the wife of a lecturer. *He* likes it; but two of that trade in one family is more than human nature can stagger under. It is enough for me to see him come home white about the gills, with a muddy valise, and a mousey horror of a travelling blanket, that I always air the first thing, and with an insane desire to indulge in a Rip Van Winkle nap, and dodge his kind. Now I hope, in conclusion, it is sufficiently clear to you that I have no call on the platform. My "sphere is home." I trust Dr. Holland will make a note of this. "*My sphere is home*," especially when I'm asked to do anything outside of it that I don't want to do!

fresh air; and that is a luxury that is always denied to lecturers. They'll applaud him, and they'll ask him "what he'll drink," and they'll take him to execution in a carriage, and take his corpse back in a carriage, but they won't let him breathe, at least till they've done with him, and I shouldn't long survive such politeness. Then the stereotyped pitcher of water would close my lips instead of helping to open them. I hate a pitcher of water. I got a boxed ear for saying that once; but I've got two ears, that's a comfort, so I'll say it again. Then, I couldn't lecture because I should feel cold shivers down my back, when that awful chairman rose and said, "Ladies and gentlemen, allow me to introduce to you the speaker for this evening, FANNY FERN." I hate that. I should want to hop up and speak when I got ready—say—while the lovers in the audience were whispering to each other, and the old ladies settling where to put their "umberils," and the old gentlemen hunting their pockets for their "spettacles" which they had left at home, and the old maids trying to find a seat where "a horrid man" wasn't too near. I'd like to pounce on them, like a cat, just then, and give my first scratch and draw blood; and then they'd let me go on my own way; because, you see, I am one of those persons who can't do anything "to order." I often see in the papers advertisements of "shirts made—to order," but I never yet saw an advertisement of a corresponding female garment made that way. Did you? Well, that's a hint that females shouldn't be hampered by stupid rules and precedents. But this is a digression.

Again, I couldn't lecture because I can't bear saleratus, and I suppose all my engagements wouldn't be in cities. Then, nextly, I couldn't lecture, because, after the lecture was over, I should be "dead beat;" and that is just the time everybody would hurry into the committee-room to tell me that I was; and to use a dozen dictionaries, to advise "me not to talk," but to go right straight home and go to bed as soon—as *they* had got through talking with me!

Lastly, the reason I can't lecture is because I am the wife of a lecturer. *He* likes it; but two of that trade in one family is more than human nature can stagger under. It is enough for me to see him come home white about the gills, with a muddy valise, and a mousey horror of a travelling blanket, that I always air the first thing, and with an insane desire to indulge in a Rip Van Winkle nap, and dodge his kind. Now I hope, in conclusion, it is sufficiently clear to you that I have no call on the platform. My "sphere is home." I trust Dr. Holland will make a note of this. "*My sphere is home*," especially when I'm asked to do anything outside of it that I don't want to do!

IN THE CARS.

"PALACE cars" are a great invention for mothers with uneasy babies, for invalids, and for lovers. But as I am in neither of the above positions, allow me to express a preference for a seat in the common car. If I *am* to eat in public out of my luncheon basket, I prefer a large audience, with their backs to me, to a small one employed in looking down my throat. Then if I wish to go to sleep, again the audience have their backs to me. Or if I wish to read, they are not holding a coroner's inquest on my politics, or my literary taste in books. Then, again, although *I* want to pass unnoticed, yet with the lovely consistency of human nature generally, I like to observe life around me, and have enough of it to observe, too.

One result of my observations in this line has been the necessity of supporting a travelling missionary, to take from the necks of little children, in a hot car, the woollen mufflers that are turning their faces brick red, and the woollen mittens that are driving them wild, while their fond parents are absorbed in looking at illustrated papers, to get a snatched *free* reading before the carrier returns for the same. It is very funny how they will let these children wriggle and twist and turn, like little worms, and never think that anything can be the matter, save a lack of peanuts or painted lozenges, which they procure with a fiendish haste, and bestow with a profusion astounding to gods and *some* women. Presently the little victims call for "a drink of water," as well they may, with their feverish throats and mouths; but that only makes matters worse; so, by way of assuagement, a wedge of mince-pie is added, or a huge doughnut, supplemented by parched corn.

"Ye gods!" I mentally exclaim; and yet we keep on sending "missionaries to the *heathen*." I am not there at the journey's end to see how those children's ears are boxed for growing devilish on such fare, but I know it is done all the same by these ignorant parents. It is refreshing occasionally to hear a father or mother say to a child, "If you are hungry, you can eat this nice piece of bread and butter, or this bit of chicken, but you must not eat nuts, candy, pastry, and cake, when you are travelling." It is refreshing to hear one say, "Eat *slowly*, dear." It is refreshing to see one take off a child's hat or cap, and lay the little owner comfortably down for the little nap, instead of letting the child bob its tired, heated head vainly in every direction for rest. Now papa understands well enough in his own case what to do, in the way of alleviation; but children are bundled up like so many packages, on starting—labelled, ticketed—and, like these packages, not to be untied through any diversities of temperature till the bumping journey's end.

It is monstrous! I am glad they kick all night after it—if so be their parents sleep with them!

But isn't it great, when, in addition to all these inflictions, a book-vender comes round and tries to make you buy one of your own books? That is the last ounce on the camel's back! How all its shortcomings and crudenesses come up before you! How all its "Errata!" How short you cut that wretched boy in his parrot panegyric! How you perspire with disgust till he takes it out of your sight and hearing, and how you pray "just Heaven" to forgive you for your sins of commission, all for bread and butter.

Now—as the story writers say when they drag in a moral by the head and shoulders, at the end of their narratives—"my object is accomplished, if the perusal of this, etc., shall have induced but *one* reader to reform, and lead a different life!"

So *I* say, if only one wretched little young one gets his dangling legs put up on the seat; or his hot woollen tippet unwound from his strangled neck, or is refused candy and lozenges, or is fed wholesomely at proper intervals, instead of keeping up a continuous chewing all through the day; or don't get spanked afterward for the inevitable results; or if I have dissuaded but one individual from buying a book with "Fern" on its covers, my object will have been accomplished!

PETTING.

IN the course of my reading, I came upon this sentence the other day:

"I have thought a great deal lately upon a kind of petting women demand, that does not seem to me wholesome or well. Even the strongest women require perpetual indorsement, or they lose heart. Can they not be strong in a purpose, though it bring neither kiss nor commendation?"

It seems to me that this writer cannot have passed out of sight of her or his own chimney, not to have seen the great army of women, wives of drunken and dissipated husbands, who, not only lacking "kiss and commendation," but receiving in place of them kicks and blows, and profane abuse, keep steadily on, performing their hard, inexorable duties with no human recognition of their heroism. Also, there are wives, clad in purple and fine linen, quite as much to be pitied, whose husbands are a disgrace to manhood, though they themselves may fail in no wifely or motherly duty. Blind indeed must that person be who fails to see all this every hour in the twenty-four.

So much for the truth of the remark. Now as to "petting." That woman is no woman—lacks woman's, I had almost said, *chiefest* charm—who does not love to be "petted." The very women who stifle their hearts' cries, because it is vain to listen for an answer where they had a sacred right to look for it, and go on performing their duty all the same—if it be their duty—are the women who most long for "petting," and *who best deserve it too;* and I, for one, have yet to learn that it is anything to be ashamed of. If so, men have a great sin on their souls; for they cannot get along at all—the majority of them—without this very sort of bolstering up.

Read any of the thousand and one precious books on "Advice to Women," and you will see how we are all to be up to time on the front door-step, ready to "smile" at our husbands the minute the poor dears come home, lest they lose heart and doubt our love for them; better for the twins to cry, than the husband and father. Just so with advice to young girls. They must always be on hand to mend rips in their brothers' gloves and tempers, and coddle them generally; but I have yet to see the book which enjoins upon brothers to be chivalric and courteous and gentlemanly to their sisters, as they take pleasure and pride in being to other young men's sisters.

"There is a time for everything," the good Book says, and so there is a time and place to be "petted." None of us want it in public. In fact, the men and women guilty of it render themselves liable to the suspicion of *only* being affectionate in public. But deliver me from the granite woman who *prefers* to live without it, who prides herself on not wanting it. I wouldn't trust her with my baby were there a knife handy. Thank God there are few such. The noblest and greatest and best women I have ever known, have been big-hearted and loving, and have known how to pet and *be* " petted," without losing either strength or dignity of character.

FACING A THIN CONGREGATION.—It is comparatively easy for a clergyman to preach to a full audience; but the test which shows whether one's heart is in his work, is to get up and face a thin congregation, and yet deliver his message with an earnestness which shows that he has a realizing sense of the value of even *one* soul. Only that clergyman who keeps this at all times in view, can so utterly leave himself out of consideration, that he will be just as eloquent and just as earnest when speaking to a thin audience, as if he were addressing a large multitude, from whose eager, upturned faces he might well draw inspiration.

MY GRIEVANCE.

SOME jilted bachelor has remarked that "no woman is happy unless she has a grievance." Taking this view of the case, it seems to me that men generally deserve great praise for their assiduity in furnishing this alleged requisite of feminine felicity. But that is not what I was going to talk about. *I* have "a grievance." My *fly* has come! I say *my* fly, because, as far as I can find out, he never goes to anybody else; he is indifferent to the most attractive visitor; what he wants is *me*—alas! *me—only* me! The tortures I have endured from that creature, no pen, tongue, or dictionary can ever express. His sleepless, untiring, relentless persecution of a harmless female is quite fiendish. His deliberate choice, and persistent retention of agonizing titillating perches, shows a depth of "strategy" unequalled in one so young. Raps, slaps, exclamations not in the hymn-book, handkerchief waving, sudden startings to the feet—what do they all avail me? He dogs me like a bailiff, from one corner of the room to another. All the long, hot day he attends my steps; all night he hovers over my couch, ready for me at the first glimmer of daybreak. The marvellous life-preserving way he has of dodging instant and vengeful annihilation, would excite my admiration, were not all my faculties required to soothe my nose after his repeated visits. In vain I pull my hair over my ears to shield them. In vain I try to decoy him into saucers of sweet things while I write. Down goes my pen, while my hands fly like the wings of a windmill in the vain attempt to dislodge him permanently. In vain I open the door, in the hope he may be tempted out. In vain I seat myself by the open window, trusting he will join the festive throng of happy Christian flies, whizzing in the open air in squads, and harming nobody. If he would *only* go, you know, I would clap down my window, and die of stifling, rather than of his harrowing tickling. See there! he goes just near enough to raise my hopes, and then lights on the back of my neck. I slap him—he retires an instant—I throw my slipper after him—it breaks my Cologne bottle, and he comes back and alights on my nostril. Look! here! I'm getting mad; now I'll just sit calmly down in that arm-chair, and fix my eyes on that Madonna, and *let* him bite. *Some time* he will surely get enough, and now I'll just stand it as long as he can. Heavens! no, I can't; he is *inside* my ear! Now, as I'm a sinner, I'll tell you what I'll do. Good! I'll go a journey, and lose him! I'll go to Lake George. Saints and angels, don't he follow me there too? To Niagara—do the rapids rid me of him? To the White Mountains? Don't he ascend with me? To the sea-shore? Is he afraid of the seventh wave? Look here! a thought strikes me. Do you suppose that fly would cross Jordan with me? for I can't stand this thing much longer.

STANDING ALONE—Thank Heaven, *I* can stand alone! Can you? Are you yet at the end of your life journey? Have you yet stood over the dead body of wife or child, snatched from you when life was at the flood-tide of happiness? Did you ever close your weary eyes to the bright dawn of a new day, and pray that you might never live to look at another? If a woman, did you ever face poverty where luxury had been, and vainly look hither and thither for the summer friends that you would never see again till larder and coffer were replenished? Are you *sure*, when you boast that you can "stand alone," that you have learned also how to *fall alone?*

CEMETERY MUSINGS.

WHEN I am in a new place I always stroll into its principal cemetery. I fancy that the average age of the dead tells its own story of the healthfulness of the neighborhood, or the contrary. The style of monumental inscription is also a good test of its educational and moral progress. One delicious morning in July, I passed through the gateway of the beautiful cemetery in the town of ——. Little birds were pluming themselves on the moss-grown tombstones, or alighting, with eye askance, on the pathway before me, or swaying on some light branch and singing as if there were no such thing as sorrow or death in this bright world; while the sunbeams slanted down through the trees, touching the half-effaced inscriptions, as if lovingly, for the "stranger within the gate." Now and then one heard the click of the chisel, as some new name was being added to those already inscribed there; while in the distance the mowers were busy, scythe in hand, laying low the tall grass, as they carefully touched the many graves, and recited little homely histories of those whom the Great Reaper had garnered. Little children were playing innocently about, with eyes like gems, and flowing locks, and graceful, gliding steps, now and then stooping to inhale the flowers, or spell out with pretty blunders a passing inscription. Go not there, my little ones—*that* inscription is not for you—your God is love. Into His hand yours is now placed confidingly, lead wheresoever He may, to fall asleep on His bosom in His own good time. Why should *you* read, " Prepare each day the funeral shroud." Why should you fetter your simple, sweet faith in " Our Father " by chains of *fear*, through which, all your lifetime, you " should be subject to bondage " ? Why for *you* should skulls be disinterred and dry bones held up to startle and affright ? Step away, little children. Think not of " shrouds " and " coffins ; " *this* is the lesson He taught you : " Little children, love one another." When He giveth His beloved sleep, neither you nor I shall know, nor does it matter.

And as I moved through this lovely place, breathing of beauty, and balm, and the song of birds, and the scent of flowers, I said to myself, Oh why, when the warm, throbbing heart of life is so slow to comprehend the *unseen*, and so tenaciously clings to the things seen, should it have *hindrance*, instead of help, in its efforts to spell out *immortality!* Why fetter it from childhood with those gloomy clogs and burdens ? How many *good* men and *good* women have struggled vainly through a lifetime with these physical, funereal terrors. And so I turned away to the graves of the " Little Annies " and " Little Freddys," where love had placed its freshly gathered flowers, and said : " *This is wiser; this is better.*"

THE SCRUBBING-BRUSH MANIA.

DID you ever see a woman who was possessed by the house-cleaning fiend? Not periodically, but at all times. Who would go about drawing her finger over every lounge, and table, and chair, speering into cracks and crannies for crooked pins and lint; holding tumblers up to the light for finger marks; in short, so utterly absorbed in the pursuit of dirt that every other pursuit was as nothing in comparison.

Now, being New England born, I know what neatness is, and value it as only a New Englander can; but when it takes such shape as this, and robs life of all its charms, I turn my back upon it with righteous disgust. Who thanks these zealous furies for their self-imposed labors? Certainly not their husbands, who flee into remote corners from dust-pans and dust-brushes, and weary of the recitals of their prowess day by day. Certainly not their children, who have no place to stow away their little sacred property in the shape of bright bits of silk or paper, or broken cups, which are dear and precious to them, and should always be held in respect within proper, innocent limits.

Oh, ye careful and troubled Marthas of the household, stop and take breath. Place a flower on the mantel, that you and your household may perhaps have some in their lives. While you stop to rest, read. So shall the cobwebs be brushed from your neglected brain, and you shall learn that something else besides cleanliness is necessary to make home *really* home for those dependent on your care.

Throw your broom out of doors; take your children by the hand, and let the fresh wind touch your wrinkled forehead. If your house is wound up to such an immaculate pitch of cleanliness, it can run on a few hours without your care. Laugh and talk with them, or better still, listen to their foolish-wise talk. Bring home a bit of gingerbread for each of them, and play some simple game with them. Put on the freshest dress you have, and ask your husband, when he comes in, if he recognizes his wife.

"I wish my mother looked as pretty as you," said a little girl, one day, to a neighbor.

"But your mamma is much prettier than I," replied the neighbor. The truth was that the child's mother always was in a wrapper, unless company was expected. The rest of the time she was under the dominion of the house-cleaning fiend, and the children fled from such a joyless utilitarian home, where no flower of beauty could ever get time to take root and blossom.

There is little need to misinterpret my meaning. Many a ruined life has come of a joyless home. Your children take to the sunlight as naturally as do the flowers. Shut it out of your houses and they will go abroad in search of it, you may be sure of that. Isn't this worth thinking about, O ye mothers? careful and troubled about many things, and yet so blind to your first and greatest duty.

CO-OPERATIVE HOUSEKEEPING.—When the millennium comes, or when women stand by one another as men do—though I'm free to say, the reason why men do it is, that when one man does anything bad, all the rest defend him, because *they don't know but they may want to do it too*—but, as I was saying, when women will stand by each other, then we will talk about "Co-operative Housekeeping." Or, when men will help their wives out of scrapes with other women, instead of running away, or "pooh-poohing" it, *then* we will talk about a dozen families living in one house. At present Mrs. Smith's boy John *will* slap your little Sarah in the face, just to show her that he is going to be a man some day. Now, there's but one common staircase, and little Sarah can't go up and down after that without a body-guard; and Johnny's pa and your daughter Sarah's pa are business friends, and "What are you going to do about it?" coolly asks Sarah's pa, of Sarah's irritated ma.

That's the idea; and Co-operative Housekeeping, allow me to tell you, is planned by bachelors and single ladies, and to them we'll leave it.

SAUCE FOR THE GANDER.

EVERY written or spoken sentence, not calculated to benefit mankind, carries with it, I verily believe, its own antidote in the shape of narrowness and bigotry.

This comforting thought occurred to me on leaving a lecture hall the other evening, where the speaker, in saying some very good things, had mentioned all female employments, save housekeeping, especially those of writing and lecturing, with utter contempt, averring that the education and training of children were the only things worthy their notice. He did not stop to explain what was to become of all the old maids and single women generally; or whether they might be excused for earning an honest support by pen and ink, or even stepping upon the platform, when they had no "home," and consequently no "home duties" to attend to; and whether, if the lecture they should deliver were as narrow and illogical as his own, the patient public might not, as in his case, be willing to *pay* and *listen*. Also, while insisting upon every woman being a mother, and desiring nothing beyond her nursery walls, not even her own intellectual progression, to qualify her to meet the questioning *youth*, as well as the dependent *infancy* of her children, I heard not one syllable from him upon the home duty devolving on the *father* and *the husband*, as to his share in their government and *home* education, which, in my opinion, is more important than that of school; nor of the cultivation of his companionable qualities, to assist in making home pleasant. Not a word did he say on this head, no more than as if these things were not binding equally on him as on the wife. As if that *could* be "home," in any true sense, where *both* did not know and practise these duties. He told us it was "of course more pleasant for women to be like the noisy cascade, and to mount the platform, than to imitate the gentle, silent rivulet, and stay quietly at home out of the public eye." As the lecturer had a home himself, and was a husband and father, and not particularly in need of any emolument from lecturing, it occurred to me that the propriety of his own absence from the "gentle rivulet" of home duties might admit of a doubt. It could not be possible that he who could map out a wife's home duty by such strict latitude and longitude, should himself have wearied of their tameness, and "mounted the platform to keep in the public eye."

What nonsense even a male lecturer may utter! said I, as I left his presence. As if there were no women, good and earnest as well as gifted, who neglected no duties while mounting the platform, but who honored it with their womanly, dignified presence, and made every large-souled, large-brained man who listened to them rejoice that they were there.

This "vine and oak" style of talk is getting monotonous. There is more "oak" to the women of to-day than there was to those of the past. Else how could the great army of drunken, incompetent, unpractical, idle husbands be supported as they are by wives, who can't stop to be "gentle, silent rivulets," but have to "keep in the public eye" as business women? Our lecturer didn't mention this little fact—not he!

LEAVING HOME FOR THE SUMMER.—There is always a certain sadness in leaving home for the pleasant summer jaunt in the country, however glad we may be to get rid of our cares. As we close the door and turn the key, the thought *will* come: Shall we ever see this home again? Have we really left it, not only for a time, but forever? Of course, new scenes and new objects soon dissipate these thoughts; and it is well it is so, or we should not gain the relief we seek; but we doubt if the thought does not obtrude itself for the moment, even in the case of the most habitually thoughtless.

MY FIRST CONVERT.

I HAVE just received a letter from a soldier, who was with us in our late four-years struggle for the "Stars and Stripes," announcing himself a convert to the renunciation of tobacco, through my ministrations on this subject. He says that "he has to thank me for the kind encouragement I have held out to him to persevere in this resolve, and for the freedom he enjoys, now that he is no longer a slave to that filthy habit; and that he shall, while he lives, hold me in grateful remembrance for the same."

Now that's encouraging, even though I shouldn't add another member to my congregation. If any other "brother" feels like "speaking out in *meetin'*" and relating a similar experience, so much the better; but in any event I shall not cease doing my best to make proselytes. "You ought to let up on a poor fellow a little," said a smoker to me not long since; "you ought to have a little charity for a fellow." Now I don't think that. My charity is for those who silently suffer from this selfish indulgence. For the poor girls, who stand on their weary feet hours behind the counters of shops, where the master sits with his feet up, smoking till their poor heads ache, and their cheeks crimson with the polluted air, roaring for them to shut the door or window if they so much as open a crevice for relief. My charity is for myself, when, seated in a car or omnibus, some "gentleman" who has just thrown away his cigar stump, places himself next to me, and compels me to inhale his horrible breath and touch his noxious coat-sleeve. My charity is for myself, when Mike O'Brien, who is in my cellar, getting in coal, sits down on the top of it, lights his pipe, and sends up the nasty fumes into the parlor and all over the house. My charity is for myself, when the proofs of my forthcoming book are sent me to read, to be obliged to hang them out of the window, like signals of distress, before I can correct them without absolute nausea. Nor am I to be mollified by the sample-package of "Fanny Fern Tobacco" once sent me. Now I felt complimented, when a little waif of a black baby, picked up in the streets of a neighboring city, was named for me; also when a hand-cart was christened ditto; also a mud-scow; but tobacco—excuse me!

I read in a paper, the other day, of an ancient institution called "smoking-tongs," constructed to hold a live coal so securely, as to admit of its being passed round the room; *women*, at that time, as an act of hospitality, used to approach their male guests with the same, and light their pipes for them. I should have liked to have had that office; but I *don't* think I should have applied the live coal to the *pipes!*

COUNTRY HOUSEWIVES.

I THINK that between country housewives and their city boarders there is a sort of antagonism, in the very nature of things, intensified, of course, when there is unreasonableness on both sides.

The country housewife rises betimes, and betaking herself to a hot kitchen, either prepares or oversees the preparing of the expected breakfast; and this not only for the boarders, but the "help," men and women, belonging to the establishment. Perhaps her husband, regarding her only in the light of a "farm hand," never speaks to her except on topics relating to the business of the household, and objects to the baby crying, which her diverted attention necessitates, as a "nuisance," while he swallows his breakfast.

Heated and worried, she sees her city boarders come down to breakfast in cool dresses and fresh ribbons, to enjoy the result of her toil, perhaps to find fault with it. She sees them after breakfast driving out to enjoy the delicious morning air, while she must iron clothes, or wash dishes, or prepare their dinner. Now don't you see in the differing positions of the two parties material for an explosion? It is no use to reply, if they had each attained a proper and high degree of civilization there would be no need of this. Remember you have to take human nature as you *find* it, and not as you *wish* to find it. *Incessant* toil coarsens and roughens, especially woman nature. It chokes the graces in the bud, and leaves only thorns and prickers. From my heart I pity such women, with not a flower in their desert lives. Still, you know city boarders had not the ordering of it; and should not, as they often are, be disliked merely for being able to lead a life of comparative ease. Ease does not always involve happiness; remember this, discouraged country housewife. *Somebody* has had to work hard for that ease, and it may be the very woman you envy and dislike for it. She has her Gethsemane with it, of which you know nothing, though she wear a smiling face. The landscape upon which she gazes may bring tears to her eyes instead of joy to her heart, as she drives away from your door, where you stand thinking of her only as a heartless idler for whom you are to toil.

Could you sit down together, woman and woman, and talk this all over, how different often would be your judgment of each other! She thinks, perhaps, of graves far away, or worse, *living* sorrows, which she cannot forget, and that will not bear thinking of, and may only be poured into the ear of " Our Father." She has learned to shut them in, and therefore you see no sign; but they are there all the same. I want you to try and remember this, because else I think many, situated as you are, make themselves unnecessary misery.

Then, again, do not call everything city boarders consider important "only a notion." If you have done making bread because your folks like pies better, try and understand that tastes and opinions may differ on so vital a point of "vittles" and digestion. If your house and its belongings are so constructed that the decencies of life are impossible, remember that because *you* "don't mind your husband or the men on the farm," your lady boarders *may*, even at the risk of being called "fussy."

To sum all up, there must be consideration on both sides. Still, the cases are rare in which farm-houses can be the best boarding-places for city people. The ideas of the two parties on the most vital questions relating to the topics I have touched upon are so widely apart, that assimilation is next to impossible. The country housewife knows much more on many subjects than her city boarder. In return, the former might often be enlightened by the latter, even on purely physical matters. But while one side starts with the "I'm as good as you" motto, and the other feels it necessary to fence this feeling at all points, the millennium of peace and good-will must of course be indefinitely postponed.

FIRST MORNING IN THE COUNTRY.

PEACE, new-mown hay, and a sniff of the sea; I'm content. "Don't the country make you sleepy?" asked a lady of me. Sleepy! why, every part of me is so wide-awake to bliss, that I doubt whether it were not a sin to sleep, lest I might lose some fine note of Nature the while. The music of the shivering leaves, swelling, then dying away so softly; the exquisite trill of some little bird near my window; the march of the waves to the shore; the soft lights and shadows on the far hills; the happy laugh of the little brown children in the hay! I'm afraid I shall quite forget "female suffrage" here! The whirl out of which I have emerged into this temporary heaven seems like a horrid nightmare, from which I have been roused to find myself encircled in loving arms, and looked down upon by a smiling face. I dare say omnibusses are still thundering down Broadway, and piles of stone, and chaos generally, reign therein; but I can scarce conceive it in this sweet hush and prayer of Nature.

I have no doubt doctors may still be found there, giving nauseous pills by the pound, and awful "mixtures" by the quart, when all their deluded patients want is hay—and fresh milk. And I suppose ministers are there, preaching about "hell," and I don't wonder at it; but if they came here, I think heaven would come more naturally to their lips. But where *is* "here"? you ask. As if I should tell you! I shall want all the fresh air for myself. I need a great deal of breath, and the world is wide. The Great Artist too decorates it all over; so that in every spot lovely flowers shall be tinted all the same, though you may never chance to light upon them; and the clouds shall be heavenly blue; and the giant trees shall spread their sheltering, graceful arms, though you may never happen to lie on the grass beneath; and the birds in their branches will have as much melody in their throats as if you had promised to come and listen. So, you see, I may be stingy of my little paradise, and not defraud you either!

It is often very oppressive to me, the sight of so much beauty, the sound of so much harmony, that none but God perhaps may ever hear or see. Nothing expresses *Omnipotence* so well to me as this: the perfect finish of every leaf and blade; nothing left unworkmanlike; even the old rocks coated with soft moss—even the decayed tree-trunk wreathed with a graceful vine. I know there are good, lovely Quakers, but God is no Quaker. The *red* wild roses from yonder hedge, advertising their presence with wafts of incense on every passing breeze, make that fact patent. The richness of the red clover and yellow buttercups, and the myriad rainbow hues on every field and hedge-row, are anti-Quaker. So that, good as they are, I'm glad they didn't make this world. I'm sure that glorious red and yellow oriole looks better on yonder branch than would a *drab* bird. I like his saucy little ways, too. But there's one thing for which I will always shake hands with all Quakerdom: they allow their women *to speak in " meetin' !"* Nothing hurts a woman like shutting down the escape-valves of talk; but men never learn that until they find them getting dangerous, and then, when a terrible explosion comes off, they wonder "*what's got into 'em!*"

A HINT TO GENTLEMEN CRITICS.—It is a pity men don't praise women when they *are* sensible in dress. Now, notwithstanding the pressure which fashion has brought to bear upon them to return to the long trailing skirts for street wear, they have courageously resisted it, and sensibly insisted upon the comfortable, cleanly, short walking skirt for the street; and yet men keep on growling all the same about minor matters of no consequence; so that women may well exclaim, "There's no suiting them; so we will just please ourselves." A word to the wise is sufficient.

CONSCIENCE KILLING.

PEOPLE seem to think that there is but one form of self-denial; and that is the "*No*" form. Now we maintain that great self-denial is often put forth, and intense mental pain incurred, in the "Yes" form; *i.e.*, the gradual acceptance of wrong-doing. Conscience killing is a slow, torturing process, and the successful muffling of the protesting voice of one's better nature is at the expense of days and nights of misery. The son, whose every perverse step away from a loving home is on his mother's heart-strings, cannot at first plant them firmly; many a backward glance, many a sigh and tear, many a half-retraced foot-track marks his downward progress. Is there no self-denial in these abortive attempts? Can he forget at once all her pure aspirations and fond hopes for her boy? Are there not kind words, more dreadful to remember than would be the bitterest curses? Can he turn *any* way, in which proofs of her all-enduring love do not confront him, and shame him, and sting him into acutest misery? Again, can the husband and father, who screens himself behind the love of wife and children, to perpetrate acts, the constant repetition of which wears away their hope and life in the process—can he, while saying "yes" to the fiends who beckon him on, be deaf to the despairing sighs that follow him, and blind to the wrecks of broken promises that lie thickly strewn around him? Does he suffer nothing in the attempt to extinguish all that is best and noblest in him? can the mother, who, stifling the voice of nature, perjures her daughter, for ambition, at the altar, face calmly that daughter's future? Are there no misgivings, no terrible fears, no shrinking back at the last retrieving moment, from a responsibility so dreadful? Can she kiss her away from her own threshold, and forget the little trusting eyes of her babyhood, and the clinging clasp of her fingers, and the Heaven-sent thrill of happiness when she first pillowed that little head upon her bosom? Can she *ever* cut the cord, strive as she may, by which the Almighty has solemnly bound her to that child for this world and for eternity? Has it cost *her* nothing in the process, this denial of her better nature? And so, through all the relations of society, wherever a sacred trust is abused, and a confidence outraged, and obligations rent recklessly asunder, there this self-incurred species of suffering, in a greater or less degree, exists accordingly as the moral sensibilities are blunted, or the contrary. The Almighty has not ordained that this path shall be trodden thornless. Coiled in it is many a deadly serpent; the balmiest air it knows is surely death-laden. Following its tortuous windings to the close, its devotee comes to no refuge, when his heart and soul grow faint, and he casts a backward, yearning glance for the holy "long ago."

THE CRY OF A VICTIM.

THERE'S eight dollars gone! If I thought it was the last time I should be cheated, I shouldn't mind it; but I know it isn't. In this case it was friendless eighteen—*female* eighteen—sole support of widowed mother and an indefinite number of small children, and all that; got her money, and turned out a humbug. I hope the recording angel will remember that in my favor. Not to speak of the man who rushed into the area to tell me that he had just had a baby—I mean that his wife had—and that they needed everything; when I immediately scooped up an armful of whatsoever I could find; and, thanking me with grateful tears, he hastened to pawn them for rum. Then there was the gifted but unfortunate artist, who had been sketching at the White Mountains and wished me to "lend him" a greenback to carry him home, because he had read my books, and because he wanted it, and because there was not another person in the world of whom he could possibly ask such a favor; oh, no! Then there was the man who looked like the ten commandments on legs, and *must* see me, if only a few moments; whose sepulchral errand turned out to be a desire to sell me some Furniture Polish, which I bought to get rid of him, and which, when uncorked a few days after, caused the family to rush into the street without the usual ceremonial hat and bonnet. Then there was the interesting child whom I brought in to feed and warm, who helped himself to several things without leave while I was looking for others. And there was the old gentleman who sent me an illegible MS. story to read and get published; whose i's I dotted, and whose t's I crossed, and for whom I furnished commas and semicolons and periods ad libitum; whose grammar I touched up, and whose capital letters in the wrong place I extinguished; and who abused me like a pickpocket because the Editor to whom I sent it thought that Dickens or Thackeray wrote quite as well as he. Then there was the young man with a widowed mother, for whom I wore out several pairs of boots "getting him a situation;" who used to lie in bed till noon, and go to it when it didn't rain, and spend all he earned in cherry-colored cravats.

Now, I'm going to stiffen myself up against all this sort of thing in future. I've done giving pennies to the little street-sweepers to buy cream-tarts with. I hand no more hot buckwheat cakes through the grating of my basement window to red-nosed little boys with ventilator trousers. I buy no more pounds of lucifer matches from frowsy-headed women at the area door, or "Windsor soap" for sweet charity's sake, knowing it to be only common brown, with a counterfeit label. I shall turn sternly away from the Liliputian venders of flimsy bootlacings and headless shawl-pins. I wish it distinctly understood that I have no use for corset-lacings, or home-made pomatum, or questionable "Lubin" perfumes in fancy bottles.

I have looked upon the humanitarian side of the question till I don't know whether to be most disgusted at my own credulity, or the perfidy of my fellow-creatures. Now let somebody else take a turn at it.

A Hint to Organ-Grinders.—It is a curious fact that organ-grinders prefer to select for their purpose that house whose windows are ornamented with statues or flowers. There is philosophy in this; since the lady who is fond of beauty and of sweet perfumes, is also fond of music. And though some of our street strains are sufficiently wheezy and harrowing, yet much of it also is sweet and soothing, and suggestive of past luxurious evenings, and of happy faces, and of hours that flew all too swiftly. But alas! for the uplifted pen, with its suspended drop of ink, at such moments! Alas! for the printer's devil waiting on one leg in the hall! Why won't organ-grinders learn where scribblers abide?

STONES FOR BREAD.

SOME of our papers publish, the latter part of every week—and a very good custom it is—a list of different preachers, their places of worship, and the topics selected for the ensuing Sunday. We often read over this list with curiosity and interest, and lay it down with a sad wonder at some of the topics selected for the sermons. We sometimes say, why *don't* they preach about something that will come home to the worn, weary, tried heart—vexed enough already with its life-burthens—instead of entangling it in theological nets, till the blessed voice that says so sweetly, "Come unto Me," never reaches the perplexed ear? We say this in no spirit of fault-finding, or dictation, but because we are *sure* that hungry souls, who every Sunday beg for bread, receive only a stone; and go away to take up their daily burden again on Monday, with faltering, hopeless step, when they might and *should* march—singing the song of triumph!

If a mother weeps over her lost babe, if a wife mourns her husband, or a father bends over a dead son, whom he thought would live to close *his* aged eyes, do you choose that time to distress them with abstract questions and transcendental theories?

No—you see before you an aching, tried heart; and you yearn with all your sympathetic nature to comfort it. Your words are few but earnest, and full of love. You go softly with them and look at the dear, dead face, which perhaps you never saw living, and say with quivering lips, "God help you, my friend." Just so, we long sometimes to have clergymen look at the dead faces of men's lost joys and hopes, and pity the bereaved, lonely hearts that want something to lean upon besides cold, dull abstractions; that yearn for the warm, beating, pulsating heart of Infinite Love, and yet *cannot* find it. Oh! what mission on earth as blessed as to teach them where and how?

"*Come unto Me.*" These words, thousands of years old, and yet never worn out! "Come unto Me." Oh, shake off the dust of your libraries, and say, as *He* said it, "Come unto Me!"

THE END.

www.ingramcontent.com/pod-product-compliance
Lightning Source LLC
Chambersburg PA
CBHW022025240426
43667CB00042B/1184